THE TALMUD
of Jerusalem

THE TALMUD
of Jerusalem

with a preface by
DAGOBERT D. RUNES

THE WISDOM LIBRARY

A DIVISION OF

PHILOSOPHICAL LIBRARY

New York

The text of these selections is based upon
the translations from the original Hebrew
and Aramaic by Professor H. Polano.

PREFACE

The *Talmud,* which may be rendered from the Hebrew as "Research," is one of the world's ten great works of divinely inspired literature. Like the Koran and other post-Judean books of holy nature, it is impossible to conceive of the *Talmud* without the *Torah,* the ancient Books of Moses. In fact, the *Talmud* is the *Torah* perpetuated.

As long as the great Solomonic Temple towered over the lands along the Jordan, the rituals, ceremonies and observances, sacrifices, commands and prohibitions made the *Torah* a living spirit in Israel. It was both state law and religious fountainhead, the guide to daily conduct and the basis of family and social structure for all the adherents of the Covenant.

But with the sudden advent of the overbearing and hostile Caesarian Empire, the sacred walls of the Temple crumbled under the Roman ram and the people of Palestine were scattered to the four corners of the world, to become the most remarkable wandering people of all time. Thrust into strange lands with alien customs to which they were forced to adjust their own deeply felt faith, the dispersed Hebrews were often and in many places bewildered as to how to abide by the laws of the *Torah,* the Covenant they had made with their Lord.

A thousand practical problems arose before the Jews of the First Century of the Common Era: problems concerning marriage and divorce and other aspects of family life; concerning personal hygiene and ritual purity; concerning civil and ceremonial law, dietary obligations and sacrificial cults; concerning the observance of holidays and festivals, the keeping of the Sabbath, the treatment of illness, the care of the poor, and so on.

5

For a hundred years and more, distinguished scholars labored to formulate a new set of laws which would reinterpret the ancient Mosaic concepts to the sons of Israel living in a pagan world.

Finally, in third-century Palestine, under the editorship of Rabbi Judah, called "The Prince," all the new writings of biblical interpretation were correlated into a volume of six books known as the *Mishnah,* or "Repetition." This became the core of the Talmud.

During the next three hundred years the *Mishnah* was supplemented by many recorded discussions or commentaries, contributed by Babylonian as well as Palestinian rabbis. Some of these were legalistic, some philosophic, some folklorist, some allegorical. These later writings, known as the *Gemara,* or "Learning," were intended to expound the *Mishnah* and to facilitate the understanding of its difficult passages.

Thus for almost five hundred years the great *hakhamim,* or sages, of Babylon, Jerusalem and other academic centers worked in setting down first the *Mishnah* and then the *Gemara,* which together constitute the *Talmud.*

By the fifth century the compilation of the *Talmud* had come to an end, but the commentaries and addenda have never ceased, even up to our own days. In the Middle Ages, the philosopher Maimonides, the commentator Rashi, and the codifier Caro were among those who brought about a renaissance of Talmudic study in Western Europe. Many sayings and parables from such Talmudic scribes as Hillel and others became proverbial in the non-Jewish world also.

The books of the *Talmud* are uneven. They range from severe theological legalism to unsurpassed beauty of legendary literature. To borrow a phrase from one of our masters, "Who would forego a walk through the forest because some of the trees are dry and barren?"

D.D.R.

CONTENTS

7

THE TALMUD
of Jerusalem

THE RABBIS

Rabbi Judah, the "Chief"

Rabbi Judah, the holy, sometimes called, by reason of his eminence, simply "Rabbi," received his education in the different colleges and from the various sources of learning open to the student in his early days. He was a man of immense wealth, and when he reached the dignity of chief or patriarch, he expended a great portion of his riches in the assistance and for the benefit of the poor. His authority among his contemporaries was superior to that allowed any of his predecessors. He commanded both their love and respect, and it is said that no man, since the time of Moses, combined such advanced learning with authority and dignity equal to his. He was, too, like Moses, truly modest and careful to avoid all pomp and display of power.

He had his chair placed near the entrance of his lecture-room, to spare his hearers the necessity of rising while he passed among them, an honor exacted by the other chiefs. Through his influence with Antoninus, his people were permitted to study the law publicly and were granted many privileges previously denied them, and immunity from many persecutions under which they had previously suffered. It was while he occupied his high position in favor and affluence, that he collected the opinions and debates of preceding Rabbis, now forming the *Mishna*.

The emperor once sent a valuable diamond to **Rabbi**

11

Judah, requesting a token of friendship in return. The Rabbi sent him a *Mezuzah*.*

"My friend," said the emperor, "this gift of thine is of small value, compared to the rich offering which I despatched to thee."

"There *is* a difference between my gift and thine," returned the Rabbi. "That which thou gavest to me I must watch and guard lest it be stolen from me; but this which I send will watch and guard over thee, even as it is written, 'When thou walkest it will lead thee, and when thou liest down it will watch over thee.' "

Rabbi Judah desired to wed the widow of Rabbi Eleazer, and he sent a messenger to her charged with his proposals. The answer which she returned thereto was this:

"Shall a vessel once used for holy purposes be now used for those less sacred?" Implying that Rabbi Eleazer, the son of Simon, had been a greater man than was Rabbi Judah. Her answer was of the same import as the proverb, "Shall the shepherd hang his work vessels where the master of the house hung his ornaments?"

On receiving this answer Rabbi Judah sent another message to her.

"You are right," said he; "your husband was a more learned scholar than am I, but in good deeds I am at least his equal."

The widow replied:

"Still we differ; I know not that my husband was more learned than Rabbi Judah, but he was his superior in righteousness."

But was Rabbi Eleazer the superior of Rabbi Judah in learning?

* A strip of parchment inscribed with verses from the Pentateuch (Deut. 6: 4-10, and Deut. 11: 13-22), so arranged as to be placed upon the door-posts of a house in compliance with the scriptural injunction.

It was the custom in the colleges for the teachers and learned Rabbis to sit upon elevated chairs while the pupils were seated on benches, near the floor. When Rabbi Simon, the son of Gamliel, Rabbi Joshua, the son of Korcha, and other celebrated Rabbis were occupying the chairs, Rabbi Eleazer, the son of Simon, and Rabbi Judah were sitting near the floor. Rabbi Simon, son of Gamliel, the father of Rabbi Judah, desiring that some mark of distinction should be paid to his son, induced the teachers to elevate him to one of the chairs. This was done; and then Rabbi Joshua spoke, saying, "He who hath a father to speak for him may live; but he who hath none, may do the best he can, and die."

On hearing this the Rabbis elevated Rabbi Eleazer, the son of Rabbi Simon, also, but Rabbi Eleazer felt himself slighted and neglected, because the above words were spoken previous to his elevation, and said, "Is Rabbi Judah better than I?"

Never after did he feel friendly towards Rabbi Judah. Previously he had assisted the latter in preparing questions to be laid before the college, but now he made light of Judah's inquiries, saying, "They are not worthy of being considered."

This treatment was very trying to the feelings of Rabbi Judah, and he complained to his father of the insults to which he was subjected.

"Be not displeased, my son," replied the latter, "nor take umbrage at the words of Eleazer. Behold, he is a lion, and the son of a lion (a most learned man, and the son of a most learned man), whilst thou art a lion, but the son of a fox (a learned man thyself, but not possessing a learned father), therefore he is thy superior."

This is probably the reason why Rabbi Judah has said, "The world has seen three meek men—my father, the sons of Bethéra, and Jonathan, the son of Saul."

The sons of Bethera vacated their positions as chiefs of the college in favor of Hillel, pronouncing him a man of superior learning, therefore their meekness. Jonathan, the son of Saul, said to David, "Thou shalt reign over Israel, and I shall be a second to thee," therefore his meekness; and Rabbi Simon, the son of Gamliel, because he called himself a fox.

Rabbi Judah suffered greatly from bodily pain for thirteen years previous to his death, and when he felt his end on earth approaching he called his children to him and spoke to them as follows:

"Obey the voice of your mother, oh, my children, and remember the teachings of the Most High. Keep a light burning in my room, and let Joseph, the Ophnite, and Simon, the Ephraimite, faithful servants to me in my life, attend me also in my death. And now, my children, let me see the sages of Israel once more."

When the sages entered, according to his request, he said:

"Let no orations or eulogies be made for me in the cities. Open my college, and continue your holy duties thirty days after my death. Although my son Simon is a man of wisdom and understanding, yet I desire that my son Gamliel shall be my successor. Chaninah, the son of Chamah, shall sit in the second seat, next to the chief. I weep that I may study God's law no more."

Then he raised his two hands towards heaven, and said:

"Oh, Lord God of the universe, Thou knowest whether I have worked faithfully with these hands for Thy glory, to obtain a knowledge of Thy law. May it be acceptable to Thee, oh, Sovereign of the universe, that I may rest in peace."

On the day of the Rabbi's death the Rabbins proclaimed a fast, and a day of prayer, for their beloved chief. They also forbid any announcement of his death to interrupt their devotion, and they continued praying until a signal was thrown from the Rabbi's house; they all experienced a shock, as though a heavy missile had struck them, and ceased praying.

Rabbi Judah was buried on the eve of Sabbath; with him died the meekness among the people, and the fear of God.

It is said that the Rabbi had a servant who was richer than the emperor. He acquired his wealth from the sale of the litter from the Rabbi's stables, which gives some idea of the number of animals Rabbi Judah possessed.

Simon, the Righteous

Simon was performing the functions of High Priest during the triumphal career of Alexander, about the year 3000. The sons of Judah found no cause to oppose this warrior, and when, after his first victories over the Persian army, he came to Syria on his way to Egypt, they joined with the kingdoms which paid him homage.

Simon the Righteous, as representative of the nation, proceeded to the seacoast to greet the conqueror, attired in his priestly robes, and attended by a number of priests and nobles in the full dignity of their costumes.

Alexander at once approached the High Priest and greeted him warmly; and when his officers expressed their astonishment at this mark of condescension, he told them that the form and feature of this same priest, clad in the same robes he now wore, had appeared to him in a dream and promised him success in arms.

Alexander was conducted through the Temple by Simon. On entering, he said, "Blessed be the Lord of this house." He was charmed with the beauty of the structure, and expressed a desire to have a statue of himself erected as a remembrance, between the porch and the altar. Simon informed him that it was not allowable to erect any statue or image within the Temple walls, but promised that, as a remembrance, the males born among his people that year should be called Alexander. That is the manner in which the Rabbis Alexander obtained their names.

Alexander continued well-disposed towards the High Priest, and through his intercessions granted the Jews religious freedom and release from all tributary burden during the Sabbatic year; and the Jews entered Alexander's army, and assisted in his conquests.

This state of affairs lasted unfortunately only until the death of Alexander. In the quarrels among his generals, which followed and continued for two decades, the Jewish people suffered much. The armies of Antigonus and his son Demetrius destroyed the fertile fields, gave wings to blessed peace, and filled the inhabitants of Judea with horror and dismay.

'Twas on the Sabbath that Jerusalem was taken by storm. The mighty walls, impenetrable strongholds since the days of Nehemiah, were again breached and broken, and the city laid open to her enemies.

These occurrences Simon lived to see, and his trust in God as well as his love for his people were sorely tried. Yet he did not waver in his faith. He fortified the Temple, repaired its damaged places, and raised the foundation of the five courts. He enlarged the water reservoir in the Temple to provide against a scarcity during siege times, and ever after that the Temple was well supplied with water; a matter of note considering the climate and the soil of Jerusalem.

Neither did Simon neglect the spiritual interests of his people. He did not lead them to believe that their strength and safety depended only upon earthly means. He remembered well the teachings of his predecessors, "Upon three things does the salvation of Israel depend: on the observance of the law, upon reconciliation with God by means of grace furnished by the Temple worship, and upon deeds of benevolence."

The many wars and disturbances which agitated the period of his life were productive of much and varied evil, and the extremely pious sought, as in the days of the prophets, to withdraw from the world and consecrate themselves to God by Nazarean vows.

Simon did not approve of this, and protested against it in many ways. He made an exception, however, in one case, that of a young and handsome shepherd, whom he found to be really sincere in his desire. When the latter came to him, desiring to become a Nazeer, the High Priest questioned him:

"Why," he asked, "why do you, so young and handsome, with flowing, silken ringlets, why do you wish to hide so much beauty and destroy so much which is pleasant to the eye?"

"Because," replied the youth, "my flowing ringlets have almost enticed me to sin from mere vanity. I saw the reflection of my face in a clear stream, and a proneness to self-deification seemed taking such hold of me, that I desire now at once to consecrate my hair unto the Lord, through the Nazarean vow." *

Simon kissed the young shepherd, and said to him:

"Would to God there were in Israel many Nazareans like to thee."

Simon is renowned for his familiarity with the law, for his services as president and member of the great Senate, and for the efficient manner in which he strengthened the religious fervor of the people and participated in all their doings and institutions.

He officiated as High Priest for forty years, and himself announced the approach of his death on completing the services on the Day of Atonement. On entering the Holy

* The law concerning this may be found in Numbers 6.

of Holies upon this sacred day, he had been used to perceive, every year, an apparition in white garments, which attended all his actions in the performance of his office. On this particular day he failed to see it, and considered this fact a harbinger of his death. He died seven days after the holy day.

Posterity honored him as the most holy among men, and it has been asserted that during his life visible tokens of God's favor never ceased.

His grandchildren, however, deserted Judaism entirely, and set the example for those actions which brought upon Israel the troublous times of Antiochus Epiphanes.

It was shortly after Simon's death, and in view of the degeneracy of the people, that the pious resolved that only the priests should use the holy name of God. The four letters of the sacred name were substituted for the name itself, and the latter was only uttered by the priests when they concluded the daily sacrificial service, and pronounced a blessing on the people, and by the High Priest on the Day of Atonement.

Rabbi Ishmael, the High Priest

Rabbi Ishmael was one of the most prominent and excellent among the fathers of the Talmudical literature. His doctrines are pure, his ideas sublime, and his explanations clear and concise. He died a martyr to Roman persecution, and this end has set the seal of truth and conviction on all the actions and sayings of his life.

There is an historical immortality, as well as a spiritual immortality; Rabbi Ishmael has attained the former, and he was a firm believer in the latter. They who imagine the doctrine of immortality to be an outgrowth of man's vanity, claiming for himself an imaginary preference above other creatures; they who believe it an ancient fiction, without which no courts of law would be able to check the natural proneness of man towards evil doing, could never rise to the courage and sublimity of martyrdom. To Ishmael, common observation as well as innate principles proved the truth of his belief.

First, no atom of matter, in the whole vastness of the universe, is lost; how, then, can man's soul, which comprises the whole world in one idea, be lost?

Secondly, in all nature death is but a transformation; with the soul it is the portal to a new and higher realm.

Thirdly, our thoughts and feelings, emanating from the soul, are not of an earthly nature.

Rabbi Ishmael also advocated with energy the doctrine of man's free agency.

"When a man enters upon the path of truth and justice," said he, "God helps him forward, but when he chooses the way of sin, God says, 'I gave thee reason and free will, go thy way,' even as the trader will wait upon the customer who purchases a good and pleasant article, while to one who desires pitch or sulphur he says, 'Go, wait upon thyself.' "

Many ask, "Why does God permit so much corruption and evil?" Rabbi Ishmael answers, "Not God, but ye, yourselves, are the creators and supporters of moral evils. When a field is covered by weeds, shall a farmer complain to God? No; let him blame himself for his carelessness and neglect. Noble, indeed, is the feeling of the man who reflects that his virtue is his own work, and truely woful is the profligate who cannot but know that his guilt is his alone. 'To the pure help cometh from on high,' was the sentence which cheered our pious forefathers, and which should encourage us."

His definition of sin, too, is far beyond and above the confused ideas of many theologians.

"Sin is an obstruction in the heart; an inability to feel and comprehend all that is noble, true, and great, and to take part in the good." If man is to be freed from sin, his mind and heart must be opened to the influence of enlightenment. The power of the passions must be subdued, and all prejudice, selfishness, and self-complacency be removed.

For those who entertain the erroneous opinion that Judaism proclaims God as unforgiving and rancorous, nothing further should be necessary than to enumerate the Rabbi's classification of the effects of the Day of Atonement.

"He who violates an affirmative commandment, and repents, is forgiven immediately.

"He who does that thing which is forbidden, and repents, is forgiven on the Day of Atonement.

"He who commits a sin punishable by extirpation, or the death penalty, may be forgiven through suffering, but nothing save death may atone for the one who profanes the name of God."

What is a profanation of the name of God? According to Rab, he who borrows and does not repay commits that sin. Rabbi Abaya says, "A man who acts so that God's name is not honored in his mouth."

And Rabbi Jochanan says, "The man who has abased his character."

Why should a violation of the affirmative commandments be so easily expiated, as is generally believed, since they are so important? The Rabbi says that sin committed against man is more grievous in the eyes of God than that committed against Himself.

Rabbi Meir

"All that God made was very good."

Rabbi Simon, the son of Eleazer, uses the words "very good" in reference to sleep. "Man sleeps," says he, "and in a few hours he gains renewed strength." Rabbi Samuel, son of Nachman, said, "The incentive leading man towards women is 'very good,' for thereby households are organized and families are formed." Rabbi Hammuna was of the opinion that no more forcible meaning could be given to the words "very good" than in applying them to the ills of life, which, said he, "more than doctrines and reasonings keep men temperate and dependent on a Higher Power." Rabbi Simon, the son of Abba, applied the words "very good" to retaliation; and Rabbi Simon, the son of Lakish, to political government; but the teaching of Rabbi Meir was, that the death of man is "very good."

Judaism aims not to separate, but to unite mankind, and this was one of the great principles of Rabbi Meir's life.

Concerning the passage, "Man shall observe the law and live in it," he said, "Holy Writ says not Israelites, not Levites, not priests, but *men;* therefore the Gentile who observes the law stands on a level with the High Priest."

"Walk before every man in modesty and humility," he said further. "Not only before your co-religionists, but before every man."

Rabbi Meir was a great allegorist; it is said that he knew three hundred allegories relating to the fox alone. Of these but three fragments remain to us.

"A fox said to a bear, 'Come, let us go into this kitchen; they are making preparations for the Sabbath, and we shall be able to find food.' The bear followed the fox, but being bulky he was captured and punished. Angry thereat he designed to tear the fox to pieces, under the pretence that the forefathers of the fox had once stolen his food; wherein occurs the first saying, 'The fathers have eaten sour grapes, and the children's teeth are set on edge.'

" 'Nay,' said the fox, 'come with me, my good friend; let us not quarrel; I will lead thee to another place where we shall surely find food.' The fox then led the bear to a fountain, where two buckets were fastened together by a rope, like balances. It was night, and the fox pointed to the moon reflected in the water, saying, 'Here is a fine cheese; let us descend and partake of it with an appetite.' The fox entered his pail first, but being too light to balance the weight of the bear he took with him a stone. As soon as the bear had gotten into the other pail, however, the fox threw this stone away, and consequently he rose, while the bear descended to the bottom."

Here he applies his second saying, "The righteous is delivered out of trouble, and the wicked cometh in his stead." Each man must suffer for his own sins, and for his own guilt alone. He who follows the luminary of the night, sensuality, must perish, while the righteous one, though carrying a stone (sin), will throw it away betimes, and be delivered from death.

The libertine Elishah, the son of Abuyah, generally called Acher, a most learned man, was one of Rabbi Meir's teachers, and they frequently conversed on Biblical passages.

The people were not pleased that Rabbi Meir should so associate, and they called him therefore *Acherim,* a word composed of the letters of Meir and Acher. But Rabbi Meir referred them to the proverb, "Incline thy ears to listen to the words of the sages, but direct thy heart to what my thought is."

Rabbi Meir ate the date and threw away the seeds; he found a pomegranate, and partaking of the fruit, he rejected the rind. His generation did not comprehend him.

Acher upon one occasion said to Rabbi Meir, "Why is the law compared to gold and glass?"

"Because," replied Rabbi Meir, "it is as hard to acquire as gold is hard in substance, and forgotten with as much ease as glass is broken."

"No," returned the other, in the name of Rabbi Akiba, "the reason is this: when gold and glass are broken they may be melted and worked over into new shapes. So is it with the student of the law, though he may commit many faulty actions there is still hope and help for him."

Rabbi Meir always favored benevolence, and a care of self as well as of others. "He only is truly rich," he asserted, "who enjoys his wealth."

The passage in Malachi 2: "Many he withheld from iniquity," he interpreted as referring to Aaron, the first high priest, who was so respected that the mere mention of his name, or the thought of how he might regard a certain action were he present, prevented many from falling into sin.

A heathen once said to Rabbi Meir, "Does it seem credible that God, whose majesty you assert fills the universe, should have spoken from between the two staves in the ark of the sanctuary?"

In answer Rabbi Meir held up before the heathen a large and a small looking-glass, in each of which the inquirer beheld his image.

"Now," said the Rabbi, "in each mirror your body is reduced to correspond with the size of the glass,—should the same thing be impossible to God? The world is his large looking-glass, the sanctuary his small one."

In regard to instruction, Rabbi Meir always said, "Teach your pupils concisely?" he also said, "Let your supplications be brief"; and his exhortation to parents was, "Teach thy son an honest handicraft."

His favorite maxim was, "Be resolved to know my ways; be attentive at the doors of the law, and guard the law in thy heart. Before thy eyes be the fear of me; protect thy mouth from sinning; cleanse and sanctify thyself from all guilt and iniquity, and God will be with thee."

From the sentence, "Be attentive at the doors of the

law," Rabbi Meir declared that every scholar should have at least three teachers, and that the word "doors" possesses a peculiar idea or meaning. For instance, a person in passing the door of the house in which he passed his honeymoon, or the door of a hall of justice in which he has been convicted or acquitted, or the door of a house in which he has sinned, what different thoughts, feelings, and recollections will be awakened in him. With equal strength should the circumstances under which he studied the law be impressed upon his mind. The Israelites are called the "children of God," and Rabbi Meir never ceased to present this filial relation in its true light, filling to the brim the goblet of family happiness, and displaying it to the eyes of the people. "Jeremiah calls us 'foolish children,'" said he; "in Deuteronomy we are called 'children lacking faith'; but under all circumstances we remain 'the *children* of God.'"

Rabbi Meir's wife was good and pious as her husband.

There dwelt in his neighborhood some co-religionists who were followers of Greek customs, who annoyed the Rabbi very much. In his vexation he would have prayed to God to destroy them, but said Beruryah, his wife:

"Be mindful of the teachings of thy faith. Pray not that sinners may perish, but that the sin itself may disappear and no opportunity for its practice remain."

During the Rabbi's absence from home two of his sons died. Their mother, hiding her grief, awaited the father's return, and then said to him:

"My husband, some time since two jewels of inestimable value were placed with me for safe keeping. He who left them with me called for them today, and I delivered them into his hands?"

"That is right," said the Rabbi, approvingly. "We must always return cheerfully and faithfully all that is placed in our care."

Shortly after this the Rabbi asked for his sons, and the mother, taking him by the hand, led him gently to the chamber of death. Meir gazed upon his sons, and realizing the truth, wept bitterly.

"Weep not, beloved husband," said his noble wife; "didst thou not say to me we must return cheerfully when 'tis called for, all that has been placed in our care? God gave us these jewels; He left them with us for a time, and we gloried in their possession; but now that He calls for His own, we should not repine."

Hillel Hannasi

Hillel, "the chief of Israel," was the descendant of a renowned family; his father was of the tribe of Benjamin, while his mother was a lineal descendant of King David. He lived about a hundred years before the destruction of the second temple, and was called Hillel the Babylonian, having been born in Babel.

He was forty years of age before he left his native city to commence his studies of the law; he continued studying under Shemaiah and Abtalyon for forty years, and from then until his death, forty years after, he was chief of the college.

During the period of his life as a student, Hillel was often cramped for means to pursue his studies. There is a generally accepted legend, to the effect that upon one occasion, when he lacked the fee demanded by the porter for entrance to the college, he climbed up upon the window-sill, hoping to hear the lectures through the panes. It chanced to be snowing, and the student became so intensely interested that he was quite covered with the snow without being aware of it, and became insensible through the cold. The attention of those inside was called to his state by the early darkening of the room, and by them he was carried in and restored to consciousness.

Hillel's elevation to the presidency of the college occurred in a remarkable manner. The eve of the Passover fell upon the Sabbath. The two chief Rabbis of Jerusalem were the sons of Bethera, and they were asked to decide whether it would be right and lawful to prepare the paschal lamb upon the Sabbath. They were unable to decide the point, when it was mentioned to them that a man of Babel, who had studied under two renowned teachers, Shemaiah and Abtalyon, was then in the place, and might be able to aid their decision. Hillel was appealed to, and he met the question with such wisdom and clearness that the sons of Bethera exclaimed, "Thou art more worthy and competent to fill the office than we are," and through their means Hillel was elected chief of the college in the year 3728 A.M. Hillel was a man of very mild disposition, but he soon found in Shamai a rival of high and hasty temper. Shamai founded a college, which was called *Beth Shamai,* and between that institution and the *Beth Hillel* the controversies were sharp and prolonged, though in the great majority of the cases Hillel and his disciples had by far the best of the arguments.

Hillel's students numbered eighty; the most noted of whom was Jonathan, the son of Uziël.

Upon one occasion an unbeliever approached Shamai and mockingly requested the Rabbi to teach to him the tenets and principles of Judaism in the space of time he could stand on one foot. Shamai, in great wrath, bade him begone, and the man then applied to Hillel, who said:

"Do not unto others what you would not have others do to you. This is the whole law; the rest, merely commentaries upon it."

Many silly students were fond of asking plaguing questions.

"How many laws are there?" asked one of these.

"Two," replied Hillel, "the oral and the written law."

"In the latter I believe," said the student; "but why should I believe the other?"

Hillel then wrote the Hebrew alphabet upon a card, and pointing to the first letter, he asked:

"What letter is that?"

"*Aleph*," replied the student.

"Good," said Hillel; "now the next," pointing to it.

"*Beth.*"

"Good again; but how knowest thou that this is an '*aleph*' and this a '*beth?*' "

"Because we have learned so from our teachers and our ancestors."

"Well," said Hillel, "as thou acceptest this in good faith, so accept the law."

As an evidence of Hillel's practical mind and his thorough appreciation of the demands and wants of his day, the following enactment is of interest.

According to the Biblical laws, all debts were to be remitted in the Sabbatical year; as it is written: "At the end of every seven years shalt thou make a release; . . . the loan which he hath lent to his neighbor," &c. (Deut. 15: 1-2). This measure, intended to adjust the inequalities of fortune, and well qualified for its purpose under some circumstances, was in the Herodian age the cause of much trouble. The wealthy man was loth to loan his money to those most in need of it, fearing to lose it by the provisions of this law. To remedy this evil, Hillel, without directly abrogating the statute of limitation, ordained that the creditor might make a duly signed deposition before the Sabbatical year, reserving the right to collect his outstanding debts at any time that he might think proper. This enactment was beneficial alike to rich and poor, and became a law with the approval of the elders.

Hillel died about the year 3764.

Rashi

Rabbenu Shelomo Yitzchaki (Our teacher, Solomon the son of Isaac), generally known as *Rashi,* from the initial letters of his name, was born about the year 1040 in Troyes, France. As a lad, his progress was remarkable; he mastered the most abstruse studies without difficulty, obtaining, in addition to his great proficiency in philology, philosophy, medicine, astronomy, and civil law, a complete mastery over the wide range of Scriptural and Talmudical lore.

He commenced his commentaries upon the Scriptures very early in life, completing the work, it is said, in his thirty-third year. Before giving it to the public, however, he travelled for seven years, visiting the academies of Italy, Greece, Germany, Palestine, and Egypt, storing up for the benefit of coming ages all that an observant eye, a gifted mind, and a diligent scholar could glean.

Upon his return to France, Rashi published his commentaries on the Bible, a book which has never been superseded, and which is now frequently published in connection with the Hebrew Bible, and he supplemented the same, shortly after, with a commentary upon twenty-three of the treatises of the Talmud.

Many of his works were never published; but among those given to the world is a book of medicine, and a poem, "The Unity of God."

He died at the age of seventy-five years, leaving three daughters, one of whom became the mother of Samuel ben Meier, who edited and added to the works of his grandfather.

His eminence, his piety, and his learning became traditional with succeeding generations, and he became the hero of many legends of that nature, which minds in those early days were so ready to grasp and embellish.

It is said that his monarch sent for him upon one occasion, and said to him:

"I have prepared a hundred thousand chariots and two hundred ships; I desire to capture Jerusalem. My soldiers and officers are superior in skill and courage to those now in possession; what thinkest thou of my prospects for success?"

"Thou wilt capture Jerusalem," returned Rashi; "thou wilt reign over it three days, and thou wilt return to this city with three horses and as many men thereon."

"Take heed then that there be not four horses," exclaimed the monarch, angered at this prediction, "for if I return with even one more than thou hast said, I will give thy flesh to the fowls of the air."

The war lasted for four years. The monarch returned with but four horsemen left of all his army, and as they passed through the gates of the city a stone fell, killing one horse and its rider instantly. This brought to mind the words of Rashi; but when the king sought for him, he found that during his absence the old man had gone the way of all flesh.

It is claimed that the chair which Rashi used in the college is still in existence.

Rashi was also called *Farchi,* derived from the name of the city in which he lived, "Lunel." *Ferach* being the Hebrew, as lune is the French for moon.

In the words of the Talmud, "A righteous man never dies," and, "Happy the man that hath found wisdom, and he that hath acquired understanding."

Maimonides

Moses Maimonides, one of the greatest of Jewish commentators, and a descendant of Rabbi Judah, the compiler of the *Mishna,* was born in the city of Cordova, Spain, March 30th, 1135. His father was somewhat advanced in life when he married, and it is said that he entered into the conjugal state through having dreamed several successive times that he was wedded to the daughter of a butcher in his neighborhood; the lady whom he did actually marry.

Moses was the only child of this lady, who died shortly after his birth. His father lamented her demise for about a year, and then married again, several children being the result of this second union.

Moses displayed no love for study in his youth; a fact which grieved his father much. All efforts to induce him to become more studious failed; his brothers called him "the butcher's boy," as a term of reproach for his dullness; and finally, in anger, his father drove him from his home.

While traveling, entirely friendless, Moses fell in with a learned Rabbi, and admired his wisdom and knowledge so much that he resolved to study zealously and emulate such attainments.

Many years after this a new preacher was announced to lecture in the synagogue, at Cordova, upon a designated Sabbath. Numerous rumors of his wonderful learning and eloquence were rife, and all were anxious to hear him. In matter, delivery, earnestness, and effect, the sermon excelled all that the people had before listened to, and to the amazement of Maimonides the elder, and his sons, they recognized in the man all were eager to honor, their outcast relative.

The first commentary of Maimonides is upon the *Mishna,* and it concludes with these words:

"I, Moses, the son of Maymon, commenced this commentary when twenty-three years of age. I have finished it at the age of thirty in the land of Egypt."

Maimonides fled from Spain to Cairo, in Egypt, from fanaticism and persecution. There he studied the Greek and Chaldaic languages, becoming master of both after seven years' attention. His fame spread through the country. His scientific standing and his general knowledge were universally recognized, and his books were not only valued by his brethren in faith, but by all the cultured and enlightened of his day.

It is said that the king of Egypt appointed him as one of his staff of physicians. The enlightened men of the kingdom were divided into seven grades, each grade occupying a corresponding position near the throne of the king on state occasions. The monarch considered Maimonides so much superior to the others that he made for him a special position. This, Moses, a modest man, declined. The other physicians, however, were jealous of his high standing, and being unable to injure him openly, they endeavored to accomplish his ruin in a secret manner.

The king was taken very sick, and Maimonides attended him. Taking advantage of this, the physicians put poison in the draught which Moses had prepared for him, and then informed the king that the latter designed his death. To prove their words, they gave some of the mixture to a dog, and the animal died.

The king was grieved and surprised, and Maimonides, struck dumb with amazement, was unable to say a word.

"Death is the penalty for one who attempts to assassinate his ruler," said the king. "Choose now the mode of thy punishment."

Moses asked for three days for consideration, which the king granted. During this time he prepared a certain mixture, and instructed his pupils to have it ready and apply it according to his directions, when he should be brought home senseless. He then appeared before the king, and desired to have his veins opened. The vital artery was missed, as he had anticipated, and the result was as he had foreseen. After his recovery, he fled from Egypt, taking refuge in a cave, where he wrote his *"Yad Hazakah"* (the "Strong Hand"), consisting of fourteen divisions, typified by the word *Yad,* which also means fourteen.

Maimonides simplified the Talmudical rules and traditions, making them clear to the comprehension of all. He was the author of an exhaustive work, entitled, *"Mishne Torah,"* the "Second Law," which was eagerly copied and extensively disseminated. He also wrote many philosophical treatises leveled against atheism, and designed to prove that God produced the world from naught, and at the age of fifty gave to the world his great work, *Moreh Nebuchim* (Guide of the Perplexed), to which Rabbi Judah Charizi added an appendix.

Maimonides died at the age of seventy years, and his remains were interred at Cairo, Egypt. Both Jews and Gentiles mourned his loss. The lamentation in Jerusalem was intense, a fast was declared, the synagogues were opened, and a portion of the law (Levit. 25: 12 to end), and the fifth chapter of Samuel 1, were made parts of the service of the day.

Rabbi Amnon, of Metz

During the reign of one of the bishops in Metz, there lived a Jew in that city, who was called Rabbi Amnon. He was of illustrious family, of great personal merit, rich and respected by the Bishop and the people. The Bishop frequently pressed him to abjure Judaism and embrace Christianity, but without the slightest avail. It happened, however, upon a certain day, being more closely pressed than usual, and somewhat anxious to be rid of the Bishop's importunities, he said hastily, "I will consider the subject, and give thee an answer in three days."

As soon as he had left the Bishop's presence, however, his heart smote him, and an unquiet conscience blamed him for admitting, even in this manner, a doubt of the true faith. He reached home overwhelmed with grief; meat was set before him, but he refused to eat; and when his friends visited him and ascertained the cause of his low spirits, he refused their proffered consolation, saying, "I shall go down mourning to the grave for these words." On the third day, while he was still lamenting his imprudent concession, the Bishop sent for him, but he refused to answer the call.

Having refused several of the Bishop's messengers, they were finally ordered to seize him, and bring him by force before the prelate.

"Amnon," said the Bishop, "why didst thou not come to me, according to thy promise, to inform me of thy decision in regard to my request?"

"Let me," answered Amnon, "pronounce my own doom for this neglect. Let my tongue, which uttered those hasty, doubting words, be cut out; a lie I uttered, for I never intended to consider the proposition."

"Nay," said the Bishop, "I will not cut out thy tongue, but thy feet which refused to come to me, shall be cut off, and the other parts of thy obstinate body shall be also punished and tormented."

Under the Bishop's eye and order, the toes and thumbs of Rabbi Amnon were then cut off, and after having been severely tortured, he was sent home in a carriage, his mangled members beside him.

Rabbi Amnon bore all this with the greatest resignation, firmly hoping and trusting that this earthly torment would plead his pardon with God.

His life after this was of course to be measured only by days. The Feast of the New Year came round, while he was living, and he desired to be carried to the synagogue. He was conveyed to the house of God, and during the service he requested to be allowed to utter a prayer. The words, which proved to be his last, were as follows:

"I will declare the mighty holiness of this day, for it is awful and tremendous. Thy kingdom is exalted thereon; Thy throne is established in mercy, and upon it Thou dost rest in truth. Thou art the Judge, who chastiseth, and from Thee naught may be concealed. Thou bearest witness, writest, sealest, recordest, and rememberest all things, aye, those which we imagine long buried in the past. The Book of Records thou openest; the great *shophar* (cornet) is sounded; even the angels are terrified, and they cry aloud, 'The Day of Judgment dawns upon us,' for in judgment they, the angels, are not faultless.

"All who have entered the world pass before Thee, even as the shepherd causes the flock he numbers to pass under his crook, so Thou, oh Lord, causest every living soul to pass before Thee. Thou numberest, Thou visitest; appointing the limitations of every creature, Thy judgment and Thy sentence.

"On the New Year it is written, on the Day of Atonement it is sealed. Aye, all Thy decrees are recorded. Who is to live and who to die. The names of those to meet death by fire, by water, or by the sword; through hunger, through thirst, and with the pestilence. All is recorded. Those who are to have tranquillity, those who are to be disturbed. Those who are to be troubled, those who are to be blessed with repose. Those who are to be prosperous, those for whom affliction is in store. Those who are to become rich, who poor; who exalted, who cast down; but penitence, prayer, and charity, oh Lord, may avert all evil decrees."

When he had finished this declaration, in which he designed to acknowledge his sin and the justice of his punishment, Rabbi Amnon expired, dying fitly in God's house, among the assembled sons of Israel.

May the righteousness of Rabbi Amnon be a precious remembrance in Israel, and may we endeavor to emulate the same. Amen.

TEACHINGS OF THE RABBIS

Benevolence

According to a proverb of the fathers, benevolence is one of the pillars upon which the world rests. "The world," said they, "is sustained by virtue of three things—the law, divine worship, and active benevolence." The Pentateuch commences and ends with an act of benevolence, as it is written, "And the Lord God made unto Adam and to his wife coats of skin, and clothed them" (Genesis 3: 20); and also, "And He (God) buried him" (Deut. 34: 6). To do a person a favor, is to act beneficently towards him without any hope or desire of return, and may be practiced in two cases—to oblige a person to whom we are not under obligation, and to accommodate or oblige a person, with more trouble to ourselves and more gain to him than he deserves. The mercy which is mentioned in the Bible is that which is given freely and without desert upon the part of one to whom it is granted; for instance, the benevolence of God is called mercy, because we are in debt to God, and He owes us nothing. Charity is also a species of benevolence, but it can only be applied to the poor and needy; while benevolence itself is both for poor and rich, high and lowly. We may even act benevolently towards the dead, attending to the last rites; this is called mercy and truth. If we oblige a fellow-man, it is possible that he may, in the course of time, repay the same; but benevolence to the dead is the very truth of mercy; it cannot be returned. In three instances is benevolence superior to charity. Charity may be practiced by means of money; benevolence with or without money. Charity is for the poor alone; benevolence either for the poor or for the rich. Charity we can display but to the living; benevolence to the living or the dead.

"After the Lord your God ye shall walk." How is it possible for us to walk after God? By following his attributes and examples. The Lord clothed the naked, as it is written, "The Lord God made to Adam and his wife coats of skin and clothed them." So we must do the same. The Lord visited the sick. "The Lord appeared to him in the grove of Mamre" (which was immediately after the circumcision). So we must do the same. The Lord comforteth the mourner. "It came to pass after the death of Abraham, God blessed his son Isaac." So we must do the same. The Lord buried the dead, as it is written, "He (God) buried him." So must we do the same. To attend to the dead, follow to its last resting-place the dust of our fellows, is an act of benevolence both to the living and the dead; the spirit departed and the mourners.

Rabbi Judah said, "If a person weeps and mourns excessively for a lost relative, his grief becomes a murmur against the will of God, and he may soon be obliged to weep for another death." We should justify the decree of God, and exclaim with Job, "The Lord gave and the Lord hath taken; blessed be the name of the Lord."

Hospitality is another attribute of benevolence. It is said of Abraham, "And he planted an orchard." This was not an orchard as we understand the word, but an inn. Abraham opened his house to passing travelers, and entertained them in a hospitable manner. When his guests thanked him for his attention, Abraham replied, "Do not thank me, for I am not the owner of this place; thank God, who created heaven and earth." In this manner he made the name of God known among the heathens. Therefore he gave us an example of hospitality which we should follow, as it is written in the proverbs of the fathers, "Let thy house be open wide as a refuge, and let the poor be cordially received within thy walls." When they enter thy house, receive them with a friendly glance, and set immediately before them thy bread and salt. Perhaps the poor man may be hungry, and yet hesitate to ask for food. Even though there may be much to trouble thee, thou must hide thy feelings from thy guests; comfort them if they need kindly words, but lay not thine own troubles before them. Remember how kindly Abraham acted towards the three angels whom he thought were men; how hospitably he treated them, saying, "My lords, if I have found grace in your eyes, do not pass away from your servant," &c. (Gen. 18: 3.) Be always friendly to thy guests, then when thou shalt call upon the Lord He will answer thee.

God knows whether the hearts which seek Him offer Him all of which they are capable. During the existence of the Temple, the Lord received with equal favor the meat offering of a handful of flour and the sacrifice of a bull. So now, the offering of the poor is just as acceptable as the utmost which the rich man can afford, if their hearts are equally with the Lord.

It was said of Rabbi Tarphon, that though a very wealthy man, he was not charitable according to his means. One time Rabbi Akiba said to him, "Shall I invest some money for thee in real estate, in a manner which will be very profitable?" Rabbi Tarphon answered in the affirmative, and brought to Rabbi Akiba four thousand *denars* in gold, to be so applied. Rabbi Akiba immediately distributed the same among the poor. Some time after this Rabbi Tarphon met Rabbi Akiba, and asked him where the real estate which he had bought for him was situated.

Akiba led his friend to the college, and showed him a little boy, who recited for them the 112th psalm. When he reached the ninth verse, "He distributeth, he giveth to the needy, his righteousness endureth for ever":

"There," said Akiba, "thy property is with David, the king of Israel, who said, 'he distributeth, he giveth to the needy.' "

"And wherefore hast thou done this?" asked Tarphon.

"Knowest thou not," answered Rabbi Akiba, "how Nakdimon, the son of Guryon, was punished because he gave not according to his means?"

"Well," returned the other, "why didst thou not tell me this; could I not have distributed my means without thy aid?"

"Nay," said Akiba, "it is a greater virtue to cause another to give than to give one's self."

From this we may learn that he who is not charitable according to his means will be punished.

Rabbi Jochanan, the son of Lakkai, was once riding outside of Jerusalem, and his pupils had followed him. They saw a poor woman collecting the grain which dropped from the mouths and troughs of some feeding cattle, belonging to Arabs. When she saw the Rabbi, she addressed him in these brief words, "Oh Rabbi, assist me." He replied, "My daughter, whose daughter art thou?"

"I am the daughter of Nakdimon, the son of Guryon," she answered.

"Why, what has become of thy father's money?" asked the Rabbi; "the amount which thou didst receive as a dowry on thy wedding day?"

"Ah," she replied, "is there not a saying in Jerusalem, 'The salt was wanting to the money?' " *

---

* Salt is used to preserve meat; without salt the meat rots. Charity is to money even as salt is to meat.

"And thy husband's money," continued the Rabbi; "what of that?"

"That followed the other," she answered; "I have lost them both."

The Rabbi turned to his scholars and said:

"I remember, when I signed her marriage contract, her father gave her as a dowry one million golden *denars,* and her husband was wealthy in addition thereto."

The Rabbi sympathized with the woman, helped her, and wept for her.

"Happy are ye, oh sons of Israel," he said; "as long as ye perform the will of God naught can conquer ye; but if ye fail to fulfill His wishes, even the cattle are superior to ye."

He who does not practice charity commits a sin. This is proven in the life of Nachum.

Nachum, whatever occurred to him, was in the habit of saying, "This too is for the best." In his old age he became blind; both of his hands and both of his legs were amputated, and the trunk of his body was covered with a sore inflammation. His scholars said to him, "If thou art a righteous man, why art thou so sorely afflicted?"

"All this," he answered, "I brought upon myself. Once I was traveling to the house of my father-in-law, and I had with me thirty asses laden with provisions and all manner of precious articles. A man by the wayside called to me, 'Oh, Rabbi, assist me.' I told him to wait until I unloaded my asses. When that time arrived and I had removed their burdens from my beasts, I found to my sorrow that the poor man had fallen and expired. I threw myself upon his body and wept bitterly. 'Let these eyes, which had no pity on thee, be blind,' I said; 'these hands that delayed to assist thee, let them be cut off, and also these feet, which did not run to aid thee.' And yet I was not satisfied until I prayed that my whole body might be stricken with a sore inflammation. Rabbi Akiba said to me, 'Woe to me that I find thee in this state!' But I replied, 'Happy to thee that thou meetest me in this state, for through this I hope that my iniquity may be forgiven, and all my righteous deeds still remain recorded to gain me a reward of life eternal in the future world.' "

Rabbi Janay upon seeing a man bestowing alms in a public place, said, "Thou hadst better not have given at all, than to have bestowed alms so openly and put the poor man to shame.

"One should rather be thrown into a fiery furnace than be the means of bringing another to public shame."

The Rabbis particularly insist that we are not to confine the exercise of charity to our own people, for the law of Moses inculcates kindness and hospitality towards the stranger within our gates. Even the animals are especially remembered in his most merciful code.

Rabbi Juda said, "No one should sit down to his own meals, until seeing that all the animals dependent upon his care are provided for."

Rabbi Jochanan has said that it is as pleasing in God's sight if we are kind and hospitable to strangers, as if we rise up early to study His law; because the former is in fact putting His law into practice. He also said, "He who is active in kindnesses towards his fellows is forgiven his sins."

Both this Rabbi and Abba say it is better to lend to the poor than to give to them, for it prevents them from feeling ashamed of their poverty, and is really a more charitable manner of aiding them. The Rabbis have always taught that kindness is more than the mere almsgiving of charity, for it includes pleasant words with the more substantial help.

Meekness

We find in the Bible many instances of the pleasure which meekness and humility in the creature affords the Great Creator. The noblest of our ancestors were those who were free from self-pride.

Abraham, the pure in heart, knew well he was but dust of the earth; and when the sons of Heth addressed him as the "prince of God," he bowed down before them.

Moses and Aaron, the leaders of Israel, exclaimed, "What are we!" And Moses in place of being jealous on hearing that two of his followers were prophesying in the camp, said humbly, "Would that all the Lord's people were prophets." (Numb. 11: 29.)

When David dedicated to God's service the costly material he had gathered for the Temple, he meekly said, "Only of Thine own have we given Thee." (Ps. 37: 11.)

From the Great Eternal, Himself, we learn humility. He chose Mount Sinai from which to give His commandments: 'twas not the highest of the mountains. He called to Moses not from a lofty tree but from a lowly bush. When he spoke to Elijah, he allowed the wind to roar, the earth to tremble, and the fire to flash forth; but for His medium He chose "the still small voice."

Rabbi Hunnah said, "He who is proud in heart is as sinful as the idolater."

Rabbi Abira said, "He who is proud shall be humbled."

Heskaiah said, "The prayers of a proud hard-hearted man are never heard."

Rabbi Ashi said, "He who hardens his heart with pride, softens his brains with the same."

Rabbi Joshua said, "Meekness is better than sacrifice"; for is it not written, "The sacrifices of God are a broken heart—a broken contrite spirit, Thou, oh Lord, will not despise."

The Fear of God

The son of Rabbi Hunnah said, "He who possesses a knowledge of God's law, without the fear of Him, is as one who has been intrusted with the inner keys of a treasury, but from whom the outer ones are withheld."

Rabbi Alexander said, "He who possesses worldly wisdom and fears not the Lord, is as one who designs building a house and completes only the door, for as David wrote in Psalm 111th, 'The beginning of wisdom is the fear of the Lord.' "

When Rabbi Jochanan was ill, his pupils visited him and asked him for a blessing. With his dying voice the Rabbi said, "I pray that you may fear God as you fear man." "What!" exclaimed his pupils, "should we not fear God more than man?"

"I should be well content," answered the sage, "if your actions proved that you feared Him as much. When you do wrong you first make sure that no human eyes see you; show the same fear of God, who sees everywhere, and everything, at all times."

Abba says we can show our fear of God in our intercourse with one another. "Speak pleasantly and kindly to every one"; he says, "trying to pacify anger, seeking peace, and pursuing it with your brethren and with all the world, and by this means you will gain that 'favor and good understanding in the sight of God and man,' which Solomon so highly prized." (Prov. 3: 9.)

Rabbi Jochanan had heard Rabbi Simon, son of Jochay, illustrate by a parable that passage of Isaiah which reads as follows: "I, the Lord, love uprightness; but hate robbery (converted) into burnt-offering."

A king having imported certain goods upon which he laid a duty, bade his officers, as they passed the custom-house, to stop and pay the usual tariff.

Greatly astonished, his attendants addressed him thus: "Sire! all that is collected belongs to your majesty; why then give what must be eventually paid into thy treasury?"

"Because," answered the monarch, "I wish travelers to learn from the action I now order you to perform, how abhorrent dishonesty is in my eyes."

Even so is it regarding the dealings of the Almighty with us, pilgrims on earth. Though all we possess belongs to Him, yet He adds to it continually, in order to increase our temporal enjoyment. Should any one imagine, therefore, that to defraud man in order to present to God, what is solely His own, might be allowable, he would be rebuked by the teachings of Holy Writ, for the just God condemns the act, and calls it hateful.

From this we may then infer, for instance, that palm-branches, stolen in order to perform therewith the prescribed rites at the Feast of Tabernacles, are unfit for use by reason of the unlawful manner in which they were obtained.

Rabbi Eleazer said: "He who is guided by righteousness and justice in all his doings, may justly be asserted to have copied God in His unbounded beneficence. For of Him (blessed be His name) we read, 'He loveth righteousness and justice'; that is, 'The earth is filled with the loving kindness of God.' " Might we think that to follow such a course is an easy task? No! The virtue of beneficence can be gained only by great efforts. Will it be difficult, however, for him that has the fear of God constantly before his eyes to acquire this attribute? No; he will easily attain it, whose every act is done in the fear of the Lord.

"A crown of grace is the hoary head; on the way of righteousness can it be found."

So taught Solomon in his Proverbs. Hence various Rabbis, who had attained an advanced age, were questioned by their pupils as to the probable cause that had secured them that mark of divine favor. Rabbi Nechumah answered that, in regard to himself, God had taken cognizance of three principles by which he had endeavored to guide his conduct.

First, he had never striven to exalt his own standing by lowering that of his neighbor. This was agreeable to the example set by Rabbi Hunna, for the latter, while bearing on his shoulders a heavy spade, was met by Rabbi Choana Ben Chanilai, who, considering the burden derogatory to the dignity of so great a man, insisted upon relieving him of the implement and carrying it himself. But Rabbi Hunna refused, saying, "Were this your habitual calling I might permit it, but I certainly shall not permit another to perform an office which, if done by myself, may be looked upon by some as menial."

Secondly, he had never gone to his night's rest with a heart harboring ill-will against his fellow-man, conformably with the practice of Mar Zutra, who, before sleeping, offered this prayer: "O Lord! forgive all those who have done me injury."

Thirdly, he was not penurious, following the example of the righteous Job, of whom the sages relate that he declined to receive the change due him after making a purchase.

Another Rabbi, bearing also the name of Nechumah, replied to Rabbi Akiba, that he believed himself to have been blessed with long life because, in his official capacity, he had invariably set his face against accepting presents, mindful of what Solomon wrote, "He that hateth gifts will live." Another of his merits he conceived to be that of never resenting an offense; mindful of the words of Rabba,

"He who is indulgent towards others' faults, will be mercifully dealt with by the Supreme Judge."

Rabbi Zera said that the merit of having reached an extreme age was in his case due, under Providence, to his conduct through life. He governed his household with mildness and forbearance. He refrained from advancing an opinion before his superiors in wisdom. He avoided rehearsing the word of God in places not entirely free from uncleanliness. He wore the phylacteries all day, that he might be reminded of his religious duties. He did not make the college where sacred knowledge is taught, a place of convenience, as, for instance, to sleep there, either occasionally or habitually. He never rejoiced over the downfall of a fellow-mortal, nor would he designate another by a name objectionable to the party personally, or to the family of which he was a member.

Honor Thy Parents

The Bible makes man's parents equally deserving, with the Most High, of his honor and reverence. *"Honor thy father and thy mother,"* is one of the precepts of the Decalogue, and it is also written, *"Honor* God from thy wealth." *"Fear* thy father and mother," and "The Lord thy God shalt thou *fear,"* are also divine inculcations, while the penalty for the blasphemous child, who sins against either his earthly parents or the great Father of the Universe, is the same, even as it is written, "Who *curses* his father and his mother shall be put to death," and "Every man who *blasphemes* God shall carry his death."

"Three friends," said the Rabbis, "has man." God, his father, and his mother. "He who honors his parents," says God, "honors me, even as though I lived among them."

Rabbi Judah said, "Known and revealed are the ways

of man. A mother coaxes a child with kind words and gentle ways, gaining honor and affection; therefore, the Bible says, 'Honor thy father,' before 'honor thy mother.' But in regard to fearing, as the father is the preceptor of the child, teaching it the law, the Bible says, 'Every man shall fear his mother,' before the word 'father.' "

Rabbi Ulah was once asked, "How extended should be this honor due to parents?"

He replied:

"Listen, and I will tell ye how thoroughly it was observed by a heathen, Damah, the son of Nethina. He was a diamond merchant, and the sages desired to purchase from him a jewel for the ephod of the high priest. When they reached his house, they found that the key of the safe in which the diamond was kept was in the possession of Damah's father, who was sleeping. The son absolutely refused to wake his father, to obtain the key, even when the sages in their impatience offered him a much larger sum for the jewel than he had demanded. And further, when his father awoke, and he delivered the diamond to the purchasers, and they offered him the larger sum which they had named, he took from it his first price, returning the balance to them, with the words, 'I will not profit by the honor of my father.' "

Man cannot always judge of man, and in the respect paid to parents by their children, earthly eyes cannot always see the truth. For instance, a child may feed his parents on dainties, and yet deserve the punishment of a disrespectful son; while another may send his father to labor, and yet deserve reward. How may this be?

A certain man placed dainty food before his father, and bade him eat thereof. When the father had finished his meal, he said:

"My son, thou hast prepared for me a most delicious meal. Wherefrom didst thou obtain these delicacies?"

And the son replied, insultingly:

"Eat as the dogs do, old man, without asking questions."

That son inherited the punishment of disrespect.

A certain man, a miller, had a father living with him, at the time when all people not working for themselves were obliged to labor a certain number of days for the government. When it came near the time when this service would be required of the old man, his son said to him, "Go thou and labor for me in the mill, and I will go and work for the government."

He said this because they who labored for the government were beaten if their work proved unsatisfactory, and he thought "it is better for me to run the chance of being beaten than to allow my father to risk it." Therefore, he deserved the reward of the son who "honors his father."

Rabbi Chiyah asserted that God preferred honor shown to parents, to that displayed towards Himself. "It is written," said he, " 'Honor the Lord from thy wealth.' How? Through charity, good deeds, putting the *mezuzah* upon thy doorposts, making a tabernacle for thyself during Succoth, &c.; all this if thou art able. If thou art poor the omission is not counted a sin or a neglect. But it is written, 'Honor thy father and thy mother,' and the duty is demanded alike of rich and poor; aye, even shouldst thou be obliged to beg for them from door to door."

Rabbi Abahu said, "Abini, my son, hath obeyed this precept even as it should be observed."

Abini had five children, but he would not allow any of them to open the door for their grandfather, or attend to his wants when he himself was at home. Even as he desired them in their lives to honor him, so he paid respect to his father. Upon one occasion his father asked him for a glass of water. While he was procuring it the old man fell asleep, and Abini, re-entering the room, stood by his father's side with the glass in his hand until the latter awoke.

"What is fear?" and "What is honor?" ask the Rabbis.

Fear thy mother and thy father, by sitting not in their seats and standing not in their places; by paying strict attention to their words and interrupting not their speech. Be doubly careful not to criticize or judge their arguments or controversies.

Honor thy father and thy mother, by attending to their wants; giving them to eat and to drink; put their raiment upon them, and tie their shoes if they are not able to perform these services for themselves.

Rabbi Eleazer was asked how far honor towards parents should be extended, and he replied: "Cast all thy wealth into the sea; but trouble not thy father and thy mother."

Simon, the son of Jochai, said: "As the reward to those who honor their parents is great, so is the punishment equally great for those who neglect the precept."

Each precept of the Bible states what the reward for its observance will be, and with this one we are told, "In order that thy days may be prolonged, and in order that it may go well with thee."

That thy days may be prolonged, not only in this world, but also in the world to come.

The Law and Its Study

"The Lord created me as the beginning of his way" (Prov. 8: 22). This means that God created the law before he created the world. Many sages have made their lives as black as the raven, that is, cruel to themselves as the raven is to her children, by means of continual study, day and night.

Rabbi Johanan said, "It is best to study by night, when all is quiet; as it is written, 'Shout forth praises in the night.'"

Reshbi Lakish said, "Study by day and by night; as it is written, 'Thou shalt meditate therein day and night.'"

Rabbi Chonan, of Zepora, said, "The study of the law may be compared to a huge heap of dust that is to be cleared away. The foolish man says, 'It is impossible that I should be able to remove this immense heap, I will not attempt it'; but the wise man says, 'I will remove a little today, some more tomorrow, and more the day after, and thus in time I shall have removed it all.'

"It is the same with studying the law. The indolent pupil says, 'It is impossible for me to study the Bible. Just think of it, fifty chapters in Genesis; sixty-six in Isaiah, one hundred and fifty Psalms, &c. I cannot do it'; but the industrious student says, 'I will study six chapters every day, and so in time I- shall acquire the whole.'"

In Proverbs 24: 7, we find this sentence: "Wisdom is too high for a fool."

"Rabbi Jochanan illustrates this verse with an apple depending from the ceiling. The foolish man says, 'I cannot reach the fruit, it is too high'; but the wise man says, 'It may be readily obtained by placing one step upon another until thy arm is brought within reach of it.' The foolish man says, 'Only a wise man can study the entire law'; but the wise man replies, 'It is not incumbent upon thee to acquire the whole.'"

Rabbi Levi illustrates this by a parable.

A man once hired two servants to fill a basket with water. One of them said, "Why should I continue this useless labor? I put the water in one side and it immediately leaks out of the other; what profit is it?"

The other workman, who was wise, replied, "We have the profit of the reward which we receive for our labor."

It is the same in studying the law. One man says, "What does it profit me to study the law when I must ever continue it or else forget what I have learned." But the other man replies, "God will reward us for the will which we display even though we do forget."

Rabbi Ze-irah has said that even a single letter in the law which we might deem of no importance, if wanting, would neutralize the whole law. In Deuteronomy 22: 17, we read, "Neither shall he take to himself many wives, that his heart may turn away." Solomon transgressed this precept, and it is said by Rabbi Simon that the angels took note of his ill-doing and addressed the Deity: "Sovereign of the world, Solomon has made Thy law even as a law liable to change and diminution. Three precepts he has disregarded, namely, 'He shall not acquire for himself many horses,' 'neither shall he take to himself many wives,' 'nor shall he acquire to himself too much silver and gold.' " Then the Lord replied, "Solomon will perish from the earth; aye, and a hundred Solomons after him, and yet the smallest letter of the law shall not be dispensed with."

The Rabbis have often applied in a figurative sense, various passages of Holy Writ, among others the opening verse of the 55th chapter of Isaiah. "Ho, every one of ye that thirsteth, come ye to the water, and he, too, that hath no money; come ye, buy and eat; yea, come, buy without money and without price, wine and milk."

The three liquids which men are thus urged to procure are considered by the sages of Israel as typical of the law.

One Rabbi asked, "Why is the word of God compared to water?"

To this question the following answer was returned: "As water runs down from an eminence (the mountains), and rests in a low place (the sea), so the law, emanating from Heaven, can remain in the possession of those only who are humble in spirit."

Another Rabbi inquired, "Wherefore has the Word of God been likened to wine and milk?" The reply made was, "As these fluids cannot be preserved in golden vessels, but only in those of earthenware, so those minds will be the best receptacles of learning which are found in homely bodies."

Thus, for instance, Rabbi Joshua ben Chaninah, who was very homely in appearance, possessed great wisdom and erudition; and one of his favorite sayings was, that "though many have exhibited a vast amount of knowledge, notwithstanding their personal attractions, yet had they been less handsome, their acquirements might have been more extensive."

There is another reason for comparing the Word of God to the last-mentioned liquids, namely, that they demand watching, lest they be spilled or spoiled, and in the same manner our acquaintance with the Bible and the traditions requires constant cultivation, else it will be lost.

The precepts are compared to a lamp; the law of God to a light. The lamp gives light only so long as it contains oil. So he who observes the precepts receives his reward while performing them. The law, however, is a light perpetual; it is a protection for ever to the one who studies it, as it is written:

"When thou walkest, it (the law) will guide thee; when thou liest down, it will watch over thee; and when thou awakenest, it will converse with thee."

When thou walkest, it will guide thee—in *this* world; when thou liest down, it will watch over thee—in the grave; when thou awakenest, it will converse with thee— in the *life to come*.

A traveler upon his journey passed through the forest upon a dark and gloomy night. He journeyed in dread; he feared the robbers who infested the route he was traversing; he feared that he might slip and fall into some unseen ditch or pitfall on the way, and he feared, too, the wild beasts, which he knew were about him. By chance he discovered a pine torch, and lighted it, and its gleams afforded him great relief. He no longer feared brambles or pitfalls, for he could see his way before him. But the dread of robbers and wild beasts was still upon him, nor left him till the morning's dawn, the coming of the sun. Still he was uncertain of his way, until he emerged from the forest, and reached the cross-roads, when peace returned unto his heart.

The darkness in which the man walked was the lack of religious knowledge. The torch he discovered typifies God's precepts, which aided him on the way until he obtained the blessed sunlight, compared to God's holy word, the Bible. Still, while man is in the forest (the world), he is not entirely at peace; his heart is weak, and he may lose the right path; but when he reaches the cross-roads (death), then may we proclaim him truly righteous, and exclaim:

"A good name is more fragrant than rich perfume, and the day of death is better than the day of one's birth."

Rabbi Jochanan, the son of Broka, and Rabbi Eleazer, the son of Chismah, visited their teacher, Rabbi Josah, and he said to them:

"What is the news at the college; what is going on?"

"Nay," they answered, "we are thy scholars; it is for thee to speak, for us to listen."

"Nevertheless," replied Rabbi Josah, "no day passes without some occurrence of note at the college. Who lectured today?"

"Rabbi Eleazer, the son of Azaryah."

"And what was his subject?"

"He chose this verse from Deuteronomy," replied the scholar:

" 'Assemble the people together, the men, the women, and the children,' and thus he expounded it:

" 'The men came to learn, the women to listen; but wherefore the children? In order that those who brought them might receive a reward for training their children in the fear of the Lord.'

"He also expounded the verse from Ecclesiastes:

" 'The words of the wise are like goads, and like nails fastened (are the words of) the men of the assemblies, which are given by one shepherd.'

" 'Why is the law of God compared to a goad?' he said. 'Because the goad causes the ox to draw the furrow straight, and the straight furrow brings forth a plenty of good food for the life of man. So does the law of God keep man's heart straight, that it may produce good food to provide for the life eternal. But lest thou shouldst say, "The goad is movable, so therefore must the law be," it is also written, *as nails,* and likewise, as *nails fastened,* lest thou shouldst argue that nails pounded into wood diminish from sight with each stroke, and that therefore by this comparison God's law would be liable to diminution also. No; as a nail fastened or *planted,* as a tree is planted to bring forth fruit and multiply.

" 'The *men of assemblies* are those who gather in numbers to study the law. Frequently controversies arise among them, and thou mightest say, "With so many differing opinions how can I settle to a study of the law?" Thy answer is written in the words *which are given by one shepherd.* From one God have all the laws proceeded. Therefore make thy ears as a sieve, and incline thy heart to possess all these words.' "

Then said Rabbi Josah, "Happy the generation which Rabbi Eleazer teaches."

The sages of the academy in Jabnah expressed their regard for all human beings, learned and unlearned, in this manner:

"I am a creature of God and so is my neighbor. He may prefer to labor in the country; I prefer a calling in the city. I rise early for my personal benefit; he rises early to advance his own interests. As he does not seek to supplant me, I should be careful to do naught to injure his business. Shall I imagine that I am nearer to God because my profession advances the cause of learning and his does not? No. Whether we accomplish much good or little good, the Almighty will reward us in accordance with our righteous intentions."

Abaygeh offered the following as his best advice:

". . . Let him be also affable and disposed to foster kindly feelings between all people; by so doing he will gain for himself the love both of the Creator and His creatures."

Rabba always said that the possession of wisdom and a knowledge of the law necessarily lead to penitence and good deeds. "For," said he, "it would be useless to acquire great learning and the mastery of Biblical and traditional law and act irreverently towards one's parents, or towards those superior on account of age or more extensive learning."

"The fear of the Lord is the beginning of wisdom; a good understanding have all those who do God's commands."

Rabba said, "Holy Writ does not tell us that to *study* God's commands shows a good understanding, but to *do* them. We must learn, however, before we can be able to perform; and he who acts contrary through life to the teachings of the Most High had better never have been born."

"The wise man is in his smallest actions great: the fool is in his greatest actions small."

A pupil once inquired of his teacher, "What is real wisdom?" The teacher replied, "To judge liberally, to think purely, and to love thy neighbor." Another teacher answered, "The greatest wisdom is to know thyself."

"Beware of conceit and pride of learning; learn thy tongue to utter, 'I do not know.' "

If a man devotes himself to study, and becomes learned, to the delight and gratification of his teachers, and yet is modest in conversation with less intelligent people, honest in his dealings, truthful in his daily walks, the people say, "Happy is the father who allowed him to study God's law; happy the teachers who instructed him in the ways of truth; how beautiful are his ways; how meritorious his deeds! Of such an one the Bible says, 'He said to me, Thou art my servant; oh, Israel, through thee am I glorified.' "

But when a man devotes himself to study, and becomes learned, yet is disdainful with those less educated than himself, and is not particular in his dealings with his fellows, then the people say of him, "Woe to the father who allowed him to study God's law; woe to those who instructed him; how censurable is his conduct; how loathsome are his ways! 'Tis of such an one the Bible says, 'And from his country the people of the Lord departed.' "

When souls stand at the judgment-seat of God, the poor, the rich, and the wicked each are severally asked what excuse they can offer for not having studied the law. If the poor man pleads his poverty he is reminded of Hillel. Though Hillel's earnings were small he gave half each day to gain admittance to the college.

When the rich man is questioned, and answers that the care of his fortune occupied his time, he is told that

Rabbi Eleazer possessed a thousand forests and a thousand ships, and yet abandoned all the luxuries of wealth, and journeyed from town to town searching and expounding the law.

When the wicked man pleads temptation as an excuse for his evil course, he is asked if he has been more tempted than Joseph, more cruelly tried than he was, with good or evil fortune.

Yet though we are commanded to study God's law, we are not to make of it a burden; neither are we to neglect for the sake of study any other duty or reasonable recreation. "Why," once asked a pupil, "is 'thy shalt gather in thy corn in its season' a Scriptural command? Would not the people gather their corn when ripe as a matter of course? The command is superfluous."

"Not so," replied the Rabbis; "the corn might belong to a man who for the sake of study would neglect work. Work is holy and honorable in God's sight, and He would not have men fail to perform their daily duties even for the study of His law."

Prayer

Bless God for the good as well as for the evil. When you hear of a death say, "Blessed is the righteous Judge."

Prayer is Israel's only weapon, a weapon inherited from its fathers, a weapon proved in a thousand battles. Even when the gates of prayer are shut in heaven, those of tears are open.

We read (Ex. 17: 11) that in the contest with Amalek, when Moses lifted up his arms Israel prevailed. Did Moses's hands affect the war, to make it or to break it? No; but while the ones of Israel look upward with humble heart to the Great Father in Heaven, no evil can prevail against them.

"And Moses made a serpent of brass and put it upon a

pole; and it came to pass that if a serpent had bitten any man, when he beheld the serpent of brass he lived" (Numb. 21: 9).

Had the brazen serpent the power of killing or of giving life? No; but while Israel looks upward to the Great Father in Heaven, He will grant life.

"Has God pleasure in the meat and blood of sacrifices?" ask the prophets.

No. He has not so much ordained as permitted them. "It is for yourselves," He says; "not for me, that ye offer."

A king had a son whom he daily discovered carousing with dissolute companions, eating and drinking.

"Eat at my table," said the king; "eat and drink, my son, even as pleaseth thee; but let it be at my table, and not with dissolute companions."

The people loved sacrificing, and they made offerings to strange gods; therefore, God said to them: "If ye will sacrifice, bring your offerings at least to me."

Scripture ordains that the Hebrew slave who loves his bondage shall have his ears pierced against the doorpost. Why?

Because that ear heard from Sinai's heights these words: "They are my servants; they shall not be sold as bondsmen." My servants, and not my servant's servants; therefore, pierce the ear of the one who loves his bondage and rejects the freedom offered him.

He who sacrifices a whole offering shall be rewarded for a whole offering; he who offers a burnt-offering shall have the reward of a burnt-offering; but he who offers humility to God and man shall receive as great a reward as though he had offered all the sacrifices in the world.

The God of Abraham will help the one who appoints a certain place to pray to the Lord.

Rabbi Henah said, "When such a man dies they will say

of him, 'A pious man, a meek man, hath died; he followed the example of our father Abraham.' "

How do we know that Abraham appointed a certain place to pray?

"Abraham rose early in the morning and went to the place where he stood before the Lord."

Rabbi Chelboh said, "We should not hurry when we leave a place of worship."

"This," said Abayyeh, "is in reference to leaving a place of worship; but we should certainly hasten on our way thither, as it is written, 'Let us know and hasten to serve the Lord.' "

Rabbi Zabid said, "When I used to see the Rabbis hurrying to a lecture in their desire to obtain good seats, I thought to myself, 'they are violating the Sabbath.' When, however, I heard Rabbi Tarphon say, 'One should always hasten to perform a commandment even on the Sabbath,' as it is written, 'They shall follow after the Lord when He roareth like a lion,' I hurried also, in order to be early in attendance."

That place wherein we can best pray to God is His house; as it is written:

"To listen to the praises and prayers which Thy servant prays before Thee." Alluding to the service in the house of God.

Said Rabin, the son of Ada, "Whence do we derive the tradition, that when ten men are praying in the house of God the Divine Presence rests among them?

"It is written, 'God stands in the assembly of the mighty.' That an assembly or congregation consists of not less than ten, we learn from God's words to Moses in regard to the spies who were sent out to view the land of Canaan. 'How long,' said he, 'shall indulgence be given to this evil congregation?' Now the spies numbered twelve men; but Joshua and Caleb being true and faithful, there remained but ten to form the 'evil congregation.' "

"Whence do we derive the tradition that when even *one* studies the law, the Divine Presence rests with him?"

"It is written, 'In every place where I shall permit my name to be mentioned, I will come unto thee and I will bless thee.' "

Four Biblical characters offered up their prayers in a careless, unthinking manner; three of them God prospered; the other met with sorrow. They were, Eleazer, the servant of Abraham; Caleb, the son of Ye Phunneh; Saul, the son of Kish; and Jephtah the Giladite.

Eleazer prayed, "Let it come to pass that the maiden to whom I shall say, 'Let down thy pitcher, I pray thee, that I may drink'; and she shall say, 'Drink, and to thy camels also will I give drink'; shall be the one Thou hast appointed for Thy servant Isaac."

Suppose a slave had appeared and answered all the requirements which Eleazer proposed, would Abraham and Isaac have been satisfied? But God prospered his mission, and "Rebecca came out."

Caleb said, "He that will smite *Kiryath-sepher,* and capture it, to whom will I give 'Achsah, my daughter, for wife" (Judges 1: 12).

Would he have given his daughter to a slave or a heathen?

But God prospered him, and "Othniel, the son of Kenaz, Caleb's younger brother, conquered it, and he gave him 'Achsah, his daughter, for wife."

Saul said, "And it shall be that the man who killeth him (Goliath) will the king enrich with great riches, and his daughter will he give him" (1 Samuel 17).

He ran the same risk as Caleb, and God was good to him also; and David, the son of Jesse, accomplished that for which he had prayed.

Jephtah expressed himself thus: "If thou wilt indeed deliver the children of Amon into my hand, then shall it be that whatsoever cometh forth out of the doors of my house to meet me when I return in peace from the children of Amon, shall belong to the Lord, and I will offer it up for a burnt-offering" (Judges 11: 31).

Supposing an ass, or a dog, or a cat, had first met him upon his return, would he have sacrificed it for a burnt-offering? God did not prosper this risk, and the Bible says, "And Jephtah came to Mizzpah unto his house, and behold his daughter came out to meet him."

Said Rabbi Simon ben Jochai, "The requests of three persons were granted before they had finished their prayers —Eleazer, Moses, and Solomon.

"In regard to Eleazer we learn, 'And before he had yet finished speaking that, behold Rebecca came out.'

"In regard to Moses, we find, 'And it came to pass when he had made an end of speaking all these words, that the ground that was under them was cloven asunder, and the earth opened her mouth and swallowed them.'" (Korach and his company.)

"In regard to Solomon, we find, 'And just when Solomon had made an end of praying, a fire came down,'" &c.

The Sabbath

Rabbi Jochanan said, in the name of Rabbi Joseh, "To those who delight in the Sabbath shall God give inheritance without end. As it is written, 'Then shalt thou find delight in the Lord,' &c. 'And I will cause thee to enjoy the inheritance of Jacob, thy father.' Not as it was promised to Abraham, 'Arise and walk through the land to its length and breadth.' Not as it was promised to Isaac, 'I will give thee all that this land contains'; but as it was promised to Jacob, 'And thou shalt spread abroad, to the West, and to the East, to the North, and to the South.' "

Rabbi Jehudah said that if the Israelites had strictly observed the first Sabbath, after the command to sanctify the seventh day had been given, they would have been spared captivity; as it is written, "And it came to pass on the seventh day, that there went out some of the people to gather (the Mannah), but they found nothing." And in the next chapter we find, "Then came Amalek, and fought with Israel in Rephidim."

The following is one of the many tales designed to show that the observance of the Sabbath is rewarded:

One Joseph, a Jew, who honored the Sabbath, had a very rich neighbor, who was a firm believer in astrology. He was told by one of the professional astrologers that his wealth would become Joseph's. He therefore sold his estate, and bought with the proceeds a large diamond, which he sewed in his turban, saying, "Joseph can never obtain this." It so happened, however, that while standing one day upon the deck of a ship in which he was crossing the sea, a heavy wind arose and carried the turban from his head. A fish swallowed the diamond, and being caught and exposed for sale in the market, was purchased by Joseph to supply his table on the Sabbath eve. Of course, upon opening it he discovered the diamond.

Rabbi Ishmael, the son of Joshua, was asked, "How did the rich people of the land of Israel become so wealthy?" He answered, "They gave their tithes in due season, as it is written, 'Thou shalt give tithes, in order that thou mayest become rich.' " "But," answered his questioner, "tithes were given to the Levites, only while the holy temple existed. What merit did they possess while they dwelt in Babel, that they became wealthy there also?" "Because," replied the Rabbi, "they honored the Holy Law by expounding it." "But in other countries, where they did not expound the Law, how did they deserve wealth?" "By honoring the Sabbath," was the answer.

Rabbi Achiya, the son of Abah, said, "I sojourned once in Ludik, and was entertained by a certain wealthy man on the Sabbath day. The table was spread with a sumptuous repast, and the dishes were of silver and gold. Before making a blessing over the meal the master of the house said, 'Unto the Lord belongeth the earth, with all that it contains.' After the blessing he said, 'The heavens are the heavens of the Lord, but the earth hath He given to the children of men.' I said to my host, 'I trust you will excuse me, my dear sir, if I take the liberty of asking you how you have merited this prosperity?' He answered, 'I was formerly a butcher, and I always selected the finest cattle to be killed for the Sabbath, in order that the people might have the best meat on that day. To this, I believe firmly, I owe my prosperity.' I replied, 'Blessed be the Lord, that He hath given thee all this.' "

The Governor Turnusrupis once asked Rabbi Akiba, "What is this day you call the Sabbath more than any other day?" The Rabbi responded, "What art thou more than any other person?" "I am superior to others," he replied, "because the emperor has appointed me governor over them."

Then said Akiba, "The Lord our God, who is greater than your emperor, has appointed the Sabbath day to be holier than the other days."

Beautiful is the legend of the Sabbath eve.

When man leaves the synagogue for his home an angel of good and an angel of evil accompany him. If he finds the table spread in his house, the Sabbath lamps lighted, and his wife and children in festive garments ready to bless the holy day of rest, then the good angel says:

"May the next Sabbath and all thy Sabbaths be like this. Peace unto this dwelling, peace"; and the angel of evil is forced to say, "Amen!"

But if the house is not ready, if no preparations have been made to greet the Sabbath, if no heart within the dwelling has sung, "Come, my beloved, to meet the bride; the presence of the Sabbath let us receive"; then the angel of evil speaks and says:

"May all thy Sabbaths be like this"; and the weeping angel of goodness, responds, "Amen!"

Rewards and Punishments

Samson sinned against the Lord through his *eyes,* as it is written, "I have seen a woman of the daughters of the Philistines. . . . This one take for me, for she pleaseth in my *eyes*" (Judges 14: 3). Therefore through his *eyes* was he punished, as it is written, "And the Philistines seized him, and put out his eyes."

Abshalom was proud of his *hair*. "And like Abshalom there was no man as handsome in all Israel, so that he was greatly praised; from the sole of his foot up to the crown of his head there was no blemish on him. And when he shaved off the hair of his head, and it was at the end of every year that he shaved it off, because it was too heavy on him so that he had to shave it off, he weighed the hair of his head at two hundred shekels by the king's weight." Therefore by his *hair* was he hanged.

Miriam *waited* for Moses one hour (when he was in the box of bulrushes). Therefore the Israelites *waited* for Miriam seven days, when she became leprous. "And the people did not set forward until Miriam was brought in again."

Joseph buried his father. "And Joseph went up to bury his father." There was none greater among the children of Israel than Joseph. Moses excelled him afterwards, however; therefore we find, "And Moses took the bones of Joseph with him." But the world has seen none greater than Moses, therefore 'tis written, "And He (God) buried him in the valley."

When trouble and sorrow become the portion of Israel, and the fainthearted separate from their people, two angels lay their hands upon the head of him who withdraws, saying, "This one shall not see the comfort of the congregation."

When trouble comes to the congregation it is not right for a man to say, "I will go home; I will eat and drink; and things shall be peaceful to me"; 'tis of such a one that the holy book speaks, saying, "And behold there is gladness and joy; slaying of oxen, and killing of sheep; eating of flesh, and drinking of wine. 'Let us eat and drink, for tomorrow we must die.' And it was revealed in my ears by the Lord of Hosts; surely the iniquity shall not be forgiven ye until ye die" (Isaiah 22: 13).

Our teacher, Moses, always bore his share in the troubles of the congregation, as it is written, "They took a stone and put it under him" (Exodus 17: 12). Could they not have given him a chair or a cushion? But then he said, "Since the Israelites are in trouble (during the war with Amalek) lo, I will bear my part with them, for he who bears his portion of the burden will live to enjoy the hour of consolation. Woe to the one who thinks, 'Ah, well, I will neglect my duty; who can know whether I bear my part or not'; even the stones of his house, aye, the limbs of the trees, shall testify against him, as it is written, 'For the stones will cry from the wall, and the limbs of the trees will testify.' "

Trades

Rabbi Meir said, "When a man teaches his son a trade, he should pray to the Possessor of the world, the Dispenser of wealth and poverty; for in every trade and pursuit of life both the rich and the poor are to be found. It is folly for one to say, 'This is a bad trade, it will not afford me a living'; because he will find many well to do in the same occupation. Neither should a successful man boast and say, 'This is a great trade, a glorious art, it has made me wealthy'; because many working in the same line as himself have found but poverty. Let all remember that everything is through the infinite mercy and wisdom of God."

Rabbi Simon, the son of Eleazer, said, "Hast thou ever noted the fowls of the air and beasts of the field how easily their maintenance is provided for them; and yet they were only created to serve me. Now should not I find a livelihood with even less trouble, for I was made to serve my fellow-creatures? But, alas! I sinned against my Creator, therefore am I punished with poverty and obliged to labor."

Rabbi Judah said, "Most mule-drivers are cruel. They beat their poor beasts unmercifully. Most camel-drivers are upright. They travel through deserts and dangerous places, and have time for meditation and thoughts of God. The majority of seamen are religious. Their daily peril makes them so. The best doctors are deserving of punishment. In the pursuit of knowledge they experiment on their patients, and often with fatal results. The best of butchers deserve to be rated with the Amalekites, they are accustomed to blood and cruelty; as it is written of the Amalekites, 'How he met thee by the way and smote the hindmost of thee, and that were feeble behind thee, when thou wast faint and weary.' "

Death

Man is born with his hands clenched; he dies with his hands wide open. Entering life he desires to grasp everything; leaving the world, all that he possessed has slipped away.

Even as a fox is man; as a fox which seeing a fine vineyard lusted after its grapes. But the palings were placed at narrow distances, and the fox was too bulky to creep between them. For three days he fasted, and when he had grown thin he entered into the vineyard. He feasted upon the grapes, forgetful of the morrow, of all things but his enjoyment; and lo, he had again grown stout and was unable to leave the scene of his feast. So for three days more he fasted, and when he had again grown thin, he passed through the palings and stood outside the vineyard, meagre as when he entered.

So with man; poor and naked he enters the world, poor and naked does he leave.

Very expressive is the legend, one of many woven around the name of Alexander.

He wandered to the gates of Paradise and knocked for entrance.

"Who knocks?" demanded the guardian angel.

"Alexander."

"Who is Alexander?"

"Alexander—*the* Alexander—Alexander the Great— the conqueror of the world."

"We know him not," replied the angel; "this is the Lord's gate, only the righteous enter here."

Alexander begged for something to prove that he had reached the gates of Paradise, and a small piece of a skull was given to him. He showed it to his wise men, who placed it in one scale of a balance. Alexander poured gold and silver into the other scale, but the small bone weighed heavier; he poured in more, adding his crown jewels, his diadem; but still the bone outweighed them all. Then one of the wise men, taking a grain of dust from the ground placed that upon the bone, and lo, the scale flew up.

The bone was that which surrounds the eye of man; the eye of man which naught can satisfy save the dust which covers it in the grave.

When the righteous dies 'tis earth that meets with loss. The jewel will ever be a jewel, but it has passed from the possession of its former owner. Well may the loser weep.

Life is a passing shadow, say the Scriptures. The shadow of a tower or a tree; the shadow which prevails for a time? No; even as the shadow of a bird in its flight, it passeth from our sight, and neither bird nor shadow remains.

Funeral Sermon Over a Dead Rabbi

"My lover goes down into his garden, to the beds of spices, to wander about in the garden and pluck roses" (Song of Songs).

The world is the garden of my lover, and he my lover is the King of kings. Like a bed of fragrant spices is Israel, the sweet savor of piety ascends on high, the perfume of learning lingers on the passing breeze, and the bed of beauty is fenced round by gentle peace. The plants flourish and put forth leaves, leaves giving grateful shelter to those who suffer from the heats and disappointment of life, and my lover seeking the most beautiful blossom, plucks the roses, the students of the law, whose belief is their delight.

When the devouring flames seize upon the cedar, shall not the lowly hyssop fear and tremble? When anglers draw the great leviathan from his mighty deeps, what hope have the fish of the shallow pond? When the fishing-line is dropped into the dashing torrent, can they feel secure, the waters of the purling brook?

Mourn for those who are left; mourn not for the one taken by God from earth. He has entered into the eternal rest, while we are bowed with sorrow.

INCIDENTS IN THE LIVES OF THE RABBIS

Rabbi Akiba

It is man's duty to thank God for the occurrence of evil even as for the occurrence of good, as it is written, "And thou shalt love the Lord thy God with all thy heart, with all thy soul, and with all thy might."

"With all thy heart." With thy propensities towards good and towards evil.

"With all thy soul." Even though he should demand thy life.

"With all thy might." All thy personal possessions. No matter what measure be meted to thee, for good and for evil, be sincerely thankful.

Rabbi Akiba was once traveling through the country, and he had with him an ass, a rooster, and a lamp.

At nightfall he reached a village where he sought shelter for the night without success.

"All that God does is done well," said the Rabbi, and proceeding towards the forest he resolved to pass the night there. He lit his lamp, but the wind extinguished it. "All that God does is done well," he said. The ass and the rooster were devoured by wild beasts; yet still he said no more than "All that God does is well done."

Next day he learned that a troop of the enemy's soldiers had passed through the forest that night. If the ass had brayed, if the rooster had crowed, or if the soldiers had seen his light he would surely have met with death, therefore he said again, "All that God does is done well."

It happened once when Rabbi Gamliel, Rabbi Eleazer, the son of Azaria, Rabbi Judah, and Rabbi Akiba were walking together, they heard the shouts and laughter and joyous tones of a multitude of people at a distance. Four of the Rabbis wept; but Akiba laughed aloud.

"Akiba," said the others to him, "wherefore laugh? These heathens who worship idols live in peace, and are merry, while our holy city lies in ruins; weep, do not laugh."

"For that very reason I laugh, and am glad," answered Rabbi Akiba. "If God allows those who transgress His will to live happily on earth, how infinitely great must be the happiness which He has stored up in the world to come for those who observe His commands."

Upon another occasion these same Rabbis went up to Jerusalem. When they reached Mount Zophim and saw the desolation about them they rent their garments, and when they reached the spot where the Temple had stood and saw a fox run out from the very site of the holy of holies four of them wept bitterly; but again Rabbi Akiba appeared merry. His comrades again rebuked him for this, to them, unseemly state of feeling.

"Ye ask me why I am merry," said he; "come now, tell me why ye weep?"

"Because the Bible tells us that a stranger (one not descended from Aaron) who approaches the holy of holies shall be put to death, and now behold the foxes make of it a dwelling-place. Why should we not weep?"

"Ye weep," returned Akiba, "from the very reason which causes my heart to be glad. Is it not written, 'And testify to me, ye faithful witnesses, Uriah, the priest, and Zachariah, the son of Berachiahu?' Now what hath Uriah to do with Zachariah? Uriah lived during the existence of the first Temple, and Zachariah during the second. Know ye not that the prophecy of Uriah is compared to the prophecy of Zachariah. From Uriah's prophecy we find, 'Therefore for your sake Zion will be ploughed as is a field, and Jerusalem will be a desolation, and the mount of Zion shall be as a forest'; and in Zachariah we find, 'They will sit, the old men and women, in the streets of Jerusalem?' Before the prophecy of Uriah was accomplished I might have doubted the truth of Zachariah's comforting words; but now that one has been accomplished, I feel assured that the promises to Zachariah will also come to pass, therefore am I glad."

"Thy words comfort us, Akiba," answered his companions. "May God ever provide us comfort."

Still another time, when Rabbi Eleazer was very sick and his friends and scholars were weeping for him, Rabbi Akiba appeared happy, and asked them why they wept. "Because," they replied, "our beloved Rabbi is lying between life and death." "Weep not, on the contrary be glad therefor," he answered. "If his wine did not grow sour, if his flag was not stricken down, I might think that on earth he received the reward of his righteousness; but now that I see my teacher suffering for what evil he may have committed in this world, I rejoice. He hath taught us that the most righteous among us commits some sin, therefore in the world to come he will have peace."

While Rabbi Eleazer was sick, the four elders, Rabbi Tarphon, Rabbi Joshua, Rabbi Eleazer, the son of Azoria, and Rabbi Akiba, called upon him.

"Thou art better to Israel than the raindrops to earth, or the raindrops are for this world only, whilst thou, my teacher, have helped the ripening of fruit for this world and the next," said Rabbi Tarphon.

"Thou art better to Israel than the sun, for the sun is

for this world alone; thou hast given light for this world and the next," said Rabbi Joshua.

Then spoke Rabbi Eleazer, the son of Azoria:

"Thou are better to Israel," said he, "than father and mother to man. They bring him into the world, but thou, my teacher, showest him the way into the world of immortality."

Then said Rabbi Akiba:

"It is well that man should be afflicted, for his distresses atone for his sins."

"Does the Bible make such an assertion, Akiba?" asked his teacher.

"Yes," answered Akiba. " 'Twelve years old was Manassah when he became king, and fifty-and-five years did he reign in Jerusalem, and he did what was evil in the eyes of the Lord' (Kings). Now, how was this? Did Hezekiah teach the law to the whole world and not to his son Manassah? Assuredly not; but Manassah paid no attention to his precepts, and neglected the word of God until he was afflicted with bodily pain, as it is written (Chron. 33: 10), 'And the Lord spoke to Manassah and to his people, but they listened not, wherefore the Lord brought over them the captains of the armies belonging to the king of Assyria, and they took Manassah prisoner with chains, and bound him with fetters, and led him off to Babylon; and when he was in distress he besought the Lord his God, and humbled himself greatly before the God of his fathers. And he prayed to Him, and He permitted Himself to be entreated by him and heard his supplication, and brought him back to Jerusalem unto his kingdom. Then did Manassah feel conscious that the Lord is indeed the (true) God.'

"Now, what did the king of Assyria to Manassah? He placed him in a copper barrel and had a fire kindled beneath it, and while enduring great torture of his body, Manassah was further tortured in his mind. "Shall I call upon the Almighty?' he thought. 'Alas! His anger burns against me. To call upon my idols is to call in vain— alas, alas, what hope remains to me!'

"He prayed to the greatest of his idols, and waited in vain for a reply. He called to the lesser gods, and remained unanswered. Then with trembling heart he addressed the great Eternal.

" 'O Eternal! God of Abraham, Isaac, and Jacob, and their descendants, the heavens and the earth are the works of Thy hand. Thou didst give to the sea a shore, controlling with a word the power of the mighty deep. Thou art merciful as Thou art great, and Thou hast promised to accept the repentance of those who return to Thee with upright hearts. As numerous are my sins as the sands which cover the seashore. I have done evil before Thee, committing abominations in Thy presence and acting wickedly. Bound with fetters I come before Thee, and on my knees I entreat Thee, in the name of Thy great attributes of mercy, to compassionate my suffering and my distress. Pardon me, oh Lord, forgive me. Do not utterly destroy me because of my transgressions. Let not my punishment eternally continue. Though I am unworthy of Thy goodness, O Lord, yet save me in Thy mercy. Henceforth will I praise Thy name all the days of my life, for all Thy creatures delight in praising Thee, and unto Thee is the greatness and the goodness for ever and ever, Selah!"

"God heard this prayer, even as it is written, 'And He permitted Himself to be entreated by him, and brought him back to Jerusalem unto his kingdom.' "

"From which we may learn," continued Akiba, "that affliction is an atonement for sin."

Said Rabbi Eleazer, the great, "It is commanded 'thou shalt love the Lord thy God with all thy soul and with all that is loved by thee.'

"Does not 'with all thy soul' include 'with all that is loved by thee?'

"Some people love themselves more than they love their money; to them 'tis said, 'with all thy soul'; while for those who love their money more than themselves the commandment reads, 'with all that is loved by thee.' "

But Rabbi Akiba always expounded the words, "with all thy soul," to mean "even though thy life be demanded of thee."

When the decree was issued forbidding the Israelites to study the law, what did Rabbi Akiba?

He installed many congregations secretly, and in secret lectured before them.

Then Papus, the son of Juda, said to him:

"Art not afraid, Akiba? Thy doings may be discovered, and thou wilt be punished for disobeying the decree."

"Listen, and I will relate to thee a parable," answered Akiba. "A fox, walking by the river side, noticed the fishes therein swimming and swimming to and fro, never ceasing; so he said to them, 'Why are ye hurrying, what do ye fear?'

" 'The nets of the angler,' they replied.

" 'Come, then,' said the fox, 'and live with me on dry land.'

"But the fishes laughed.

" 'And art thou called the wisest of the beasts?' they exclaimed; 'verily thou art the most foolish. If we are in danger even in our element, how much greater would be our risk in leaving it.'

"It is the same with us. We are told of the law that it is 'our life and the prolongation of our days.' This is it when things are peaceful with us; how much greater is our need of it then in times like these?"

It is said that it was but shortly after this when Rabbi Akiba was imprisoned for teaching the law, and in the prison in which he was incarcerated he found Papus, who had been condemned for some other offense.

Rabbi Akiba said to him:

"Papus, what brought thee here?"

And Papus replied:

"Joy, joy, to thee, that thou art imprisoned for studying God's law; but woe, woe is mine that I am here through vanity."

When Rabbi Akiba was led forth to execution, it was just at the time of the morning service.

" 'Hear, oh Israel! the Lord our God, the Lord is one,' " he exclaimed in a loud and firm voice.

The torturers tore his flesh with pointed cards, yet still he repeated, "The Lord is one."

"Always did I say," he continued, "that 'with all thy soul,' meant even though life should be demanded of thee, and I wondered whether I should ever be able to so observe it. Now see, today, I do so; 'the Lord is one.' "

With these words he died.

Happy art thou, Rabbi Akiba, that thy soul went out in purity for the happiness of all futurity is thine.

Elishah ben Abuyah

Elishah ben Abuyah, a most learned man, became in after-life an apostate. Rabbi Meir had been one of his pupils, and he never failed in the great love which he bore for his teacher.

It happened upon one occasion when Rabbi Meir was lecturing in the college, that some students entered and said to him:

"Thy teacher, Elishah, is riding by on horseback on this holy Sabbath day."

Rabbi Meir left the college, and overtaking Elishah walked along by his horse's side.

The latter saluted him, and asked:

"What passage of Scripture hast thou been expounding?"

"From the book of Job," replied Rabbi Meir. " 'The Lord blessed the latter days of Job more than the beginning.' "

"And how didst thou explain the verse?" said Elishah.

"That the Lord increased his wealth twofold."

"But thy teacher, Akiba, said not so," returned Elishah. "He said that the Lord blessed the latter days of Job with twofold of penitence and good deeds."

"How," inquired Rabbi Meir, "wouldst thou explain the verse, 'Better is the end of a thing than the beginning thereof.' If a man buys merchandise in his youth and meets with losses, is it likely that he will recover his substance in old age? Or, if a person studies God's law in his youth and forgets it, is it probable that it will return to his memory in his latter days?"

"Thy teacher, Akiba, said not so," replied Elishah; "he explained the verse, 'Better is the end of a thing when the beginning was good. My own life proves the soundness of this explanation. On the day when I was admitted into the covenant of Abraham, my father made a great feast. Some of his visitors sang, some of them danced, but the Rabbis conversed upon God's wisdom and His laws. This latter pleased my father, Abuyah, and he said, 'When my son grows up ye shall teach him and he shall become like ye; he did not cause me to study for God's sake but only to make his name famous through me. Therefore, in my latter days have I become wicked and an apostate; and now, return home."

"And wherefore?"

"Because, on the Sabbath day, thou art allowed to go so far and no farther, and I have reckoned the distance thou hast traveled with me by the footsteps of my horse."

"If thou art so wise," said Rabbi Meir, "as to reckon the distance I may travel by the footsteps of thy horse, and so particular for my sake, why not return to God and repent of thy apostasy?"

Elishah answered:

"It is not in my power. I rode upon horseback once on the Day of Atonement; yeah, when it fell upon the Sabbath, and when I passed the synagogue I heard a voice crying, 'Return, oh backsliding children, return to me and I will return to ye; except Elishah, the son of Abuyah, he knew his Master and yet rebelled against Him.'"

What caused such a learned man as Elishah to turn to evil ways?

It is reported that once while studying the law in the vale of Genusan, he saw a man climbing a tree. The man found a bird's-nest in the tree, and taking the mother with the young ones he still departed in peace. He saw another man who finding a bird's-nest followed the Bible's command took the young only, allowing the mother to fly away; and yet a serpent stung him as he descended, and he died. "Now," thought he, "where is the Bible's truth and promises? Is it not written, 'And the young thou mayest take to thyself, but the mother thou shalt surely let go, that it may be well with thee and that thou mayest live many days.' Now, where is the long life to this man who followed the precept, while the one who transgressed it is unhurt?"

He had not heard how Rabbi Akiba expounded this verse, that the days would be long in the future world where all is happiness.

There is also another reason given as the cause for Elishah's backsliding and apostasy.

During the fearful period of religious persecution, the learned Rabbi Judah, whose life had been passed in the study of the law and the practice of God's precepts, was delivered into the power of the cruel torturer. His tongue was placed in a dog's mouth and the dog bit it off.

So Elishah said, "If a tongue which uttered naught but truth be so used, and a learned, wise man be so treated, of what use is it to avoid having a lying tongue and being ignorant. Lo, if these things are allowed, there is surely no reward for the righteous, and no resurrection for the dead."

When Elishah waxed old he was taken sick, and Rabbi Meir, learning of the illness of his aged teacher, called upon him.

"Oh return, return unto thy God," entreated Rabbi Meir.

"What!" exclaimed Elishah, "return! and could He receive my penitence, the penitence of an apostate who has so rebelled against Him?"

"Is it not written," said Meir, " 'Thou turnest man to contrition?' (Psalm 90: 3). No matter how the soul of man may be crushed, he can still turn to his God and find relief."

Elishah listened to these words, wept bitterly and died. Not many years after his death his daughters came, poverty stricken, asking relief from the colleges. "Remember," said they, "the merit of our father's learning, not his conduct."

The colleges listened to the appeal and supported the daughters of Elishah.

Rabbi Simon

Rabbi Judah, Rabbi Joseh, and Rabbi Simon were conversing one day, when Judah ben Gerim entered the apartment and sat down with the three. Rabbi Judah was speaking in a complimentary strain of the Gentiles (Romans). "See," said he, "how they have improved their cities, how beautiful they have made them, and how much they have done for the comfort and convenience of the citizens; bath-houses, bridges, fine broad streets, surely much credit is due them."

"Nay," answered Rabbi Simon, "all that they have done has been from a selfish motive. The bridges bring them in a revenue, for all who use them are taxed; the bath-houses are for their personal adornment—'tis all selfishness, not patriotism."

Judah ben Gerim repeated these remarks to his friends, and finally they reached the ears of the emperor. He would not allow them to pass unnoticed. He ordered that Judah, who had spoken well of the nation, should be advanced in honor; that Joseh, who had remained silent instead of seconding the assertions, should be banished to Zipore; and that Simon, who had disputed the compliment, should be put to death.

The latter with his son fled and concealed himself in the college when this fiat became known to him. For some time he remained there comparatively safe, his wife bringing his meals daily. But when the officers were directed to make diligent search he became afraid, lest through the indiscretion of his wife his place of concealment might be discovered.

"The mind of woman is weak and unsteady," said he, "perhaps they may question and confuse her, and thus may death come upon me."

So leaving the city, Simon and his son took refuge in a lonely cave. Near its mouth some fruit trees grew, supplying them with food, and a spring of pure water bubbled from rocks in the immediate vicinity. For thirteen years Rabbi Simon lived here, until the emperor died and his decrees were repealed. He then returned to the city.

When Rabbi Phineas, his son-in-law, heard of his return, he called upon him at once, and noticing an apparent neglect in the mental and physical condition of his relative, he exclaimed, "Woe, woe! that I meet thee in so sad a condition!"

But Rabbi Simon answered:

"Not so; happy is it that thou findest me in this condition, for thou findest me no less righteous than before. God has preserved me, and my faith in Him, and thus hereafter shall I explain the verse of Scripture, 'And Jacob came perfect.' Perfect in his physical condition, perfect in his temporal condition, and perfect in his knowledge of God."

Antoninus, in conversing with Rabbi Judah, said to him:

"In the future world, when the soul comes before the Almighty Creator for judgment, may it not find a plea of excuse for worldly wickedness in saying, 'Lo, the sin is the body's; I am now free from the body; the sins were not mine'?"

Rabbi Judah answered, "Let me relate to thee a parable. A king had an orchard of fine figs, which he prized most highly. That the fruit might not be stolen or abused, he placed two watchers in the orchard, and that they themselves might not be tempted to partake of the fruit, he chose one of them a blind man, and the other one lame. But lo, when they were in the orchard, the lame man said to his companion, 'I see very fine figs; they are luscious and tempting; carry me to the tree, that we may both partake of them.''

"So the blind man carried the lame man, and they ate of the figs.

"When the king entered the orchard he noticed at once that his finest figs were missing, and he asked the watchers what had become of them.

"The blind man answered:

" 'I know not. I could not steal them; I am blind; I cannot even see them.'

"And the lame man answered:

" 'Neither could I steal them! I could not approach the tree.'

"But the king was wise, and he answered:

" 'Lo, the blind carried the lame,' and he punished them accordingly.

"So is it with us. The world is the orchard in which the Eternal King has placed us, to keep watch and ward, to till its soil and care for its fruit. But the soul and body are the man; if one violates the precepts so does the other, and after death the soul may not say, 'It is the fault of the body to which I was tied that I committed sins'; no, God will do as did the owner of the orchard, as it is written:

" 'He shall call from the heaven above, and to the earth to judge his people' (Psalms).

"He shall call from the 'heaven above,' which is the soul, and to the 'earth below,' which is the body, mixing with the dust from whence it sprung."

A heathen said to Rabbi Joshua, "Thou believest that God knows the future?"

"Yes," replied the Rabbi.

"Then," said the questioner, "wherefore is it written, 'The Lord said, I will destroy everything which I have made, because it repenteth me that I have made them?' Did not the Lord foresee that man would become corrupt?"

Then said Rabbi Joshua, "Hast thou children?"

"Yes," was the answer.

"When a child was born, what didst thou?"

"I made a great rejoicing."

"What cause hadst thou to rejoice? Dost thou not know that they must die?"

"Yes, that is true; but in the time of enjoyment I do not think of the future."

"So was it with God," said Rabbi Joshua. "He knew that men would sin; still that knowledge did not prevent the execution of his beneficent purpose to create them."

One of the emperors said to Rabon Gamliel:

"Your God is a thief, as it is written, 'And the Lord God caused a deep sleep to fall upon Adam, and he slept. And He took a rib from Adam.' "

The Rabbi's daughter said, "Let me answer this aspersion. Last night robbers broke into my room, and stole therefrom a silver vessel: but they left a golden one in its stead."

The emperor replied, "I wish that such thieves would come every night."

Thus was it with Adam; God took a rib from him, but placed a woman instead of it.

Rabbi Joshua, of Saknin, said in the name of Rabbi Levi, "The Lord considered from what part of the man he should form woman; not from the head, lest she should be proud; not from the eyes, lest she should wish to see everything; not from the mouth, lest she might be talkative; nor from the ear, lest she should wish to hear everything; nor from the heart, lest she should be jealous; nor from the hand, lest she should wish to find out everything; nor from the feet, in order that she might not be a wanderer; only from the most hidden place, that is covered even when a man is naked—namely, the rib."

The scholars of Rabbi Simon ben Jochai once asked him:

"Why did not the Lord give to Israel enough manna to suffice them for a year, at one time, instead of meting it out daily?"

The Rabbi replied:

"I will answer ye with a parable. There was once a king who had a son to whom he gave a certain yearly allowance, paying the entire sum for his year's support on one appointed day. It soon happened that this day on which the allowance was due, was the only day in the year when the father saw his son. So the king changed his plan, and gave his son each day his maintenance for that day only, and then the son visited his father with the return of each day's sun.

"So was it with Israel; each father of a family, dependent upon the manna provided each day by God's bounty, for his support and the support of his family, naturally had his mind devoted to the Great Giver and Sustainer of life."

When Rabbi Eleazer was sick his scholars visited him, and said, "Rabbi, teach us the way of life, that we may inherit eternity."

The Rabbi answered, "Give honor to your comrades. Know to whom you pray. Restrain your children from frivolous conversation, and place them among the learned men, in order that they may acquire wisdom. So may you merit life in the future world."

When Rabbi Jochanan was sick his scholars also called upon him. When he beheld them he burst into tears.

"Rabbi!" they exclaimed, "Light of Israel! The chief pillar! Why weep?"

The Rabbi answered, "Were I to be brought before a king of flesh and blood, who is here today and tomorrow in the grave; who may be angry with me, but not for ever; who may imprison me, but not for ever; who may kill me, but only for this world; whom I may sometimes bribe; even then I would fear. But now, I am to appear before the King of kings, the Most Holy One, blessed be He, who lives through all eternity. If He is wroth, it is for ever; if He imprisons me, it is for ever; if He slays me, it is for the future world; and I can bribe Him neither with words nor money. Not only this, two paths are before me, one leading to punishment, the other to reward, and I know not which one I must travel. Should I not weep?"

The scholars of Rabbi Johanan, the son of Zakai, asked of their teacher this question:

"Wherefore is it, that according to the law, the punishment of a highwayman is not as severe as the punishment of a sneak thief? According to the Mosaic law, if a man steals an ox or a sheep, and kills it or sells it, he is required to restore five oxen for the one ox, and four sheep for the one sheep (Exodus 21: 37); but for the highwayman we find, 'When he hath sinned and is conscious of his guilt, he shall restore that he hath taken violently away; he shall restore it and its principal, and the fifth part thereof he shall add thereto.' Therefore, he who commits a highway robbery pays as punishment one-fifth of the same, while a sneak thief is obliged to return five oxen for one ox, and four sheep for one sheep. Wherefore is this?"

"Because," replied the teacher, "the highway robber

treats the servant as the master. He takes away violently in the presence of the servant, the despoiled man, and the master—God. But the sneak thief imagines that God's eye is not upon him. He acts secretly, thinking, as the Psalmist says, 'The Lord doth not see, neither will the God of Jacob regard it' (Ps. 94: 5). Listen to a parable. Two men made a feast. One invited all the inhabitants of the city, and omitted inviting the king. The other invited neither the king nor his subjects. Which one deserves condemnation? Certainly the one who invited the subjects and not the king. The people of the earth are God's subjects. The sneak thief fears their eyes, yet he does not honor the eye of the king, the eye of God, which watches all his actions."

Rabbi Meir says, "This law teaches us how God regards industry. If a person steals an ox he must return five in its place, because while the animal was in his unlawful possession it could not work for its rightful owner. A lamb, however, does no labor, and is not profitable that way; therefore he is only obliged to replace it fourfold."

Rabbi Nachman dined with his teacher, Rabbi Yitzchak, and, upon departing after the meal, he said, "Teacher, bless me!"

"Listen," replied Rabbi Yitzchak. "A traveler was once journeying through the desert, and when weary, hungry, and thirsty, he happened upon an oasis, where grew a fruitful tree, wide-branched, and at the foot of which there gushed a spring of clear, cool water.

"The stranger ate of the luscious fruit, enjoying and resting in the grateful shade, and quenching his thirst in the sparkling water which bubbled merrily at his feet.

"When about to resume his journey, he addressed the tree and spoke as follows:

" 'Oh, gracious tree, with what words can I bless thee, and what good can I wish thee? I cannot wish thee good fruit, for it is already thine; the blessing of water is also thine, and the gracious shade thrown by thy beauteous branches the Eternal has already granted thee, for my good and the good of those who travel by this way. Let me pray to God, then, that all thy offspring may be goodly as thyself.'

"So it is with thee, my pupil. How shall I bless thee? Thou art perfect in the law, eminent in the land, respected, and blessed with means. May God grant that all thy offspring may prove goodly as thyself."

A wise man, say the Rabbis, was Gebiah ben Pesisah. When the children of Canaan accused the Israelites of stealing their land, saying, "The land of Canaan is ours, as it is written, 'The land of Canaan and its boundaries belong to the Canaanites,' " and demanded restitution, Gebiah offered to argue the case before the ruler.

Said Gebiah to the Africans, "Ye bring your proof from the Pentateuch, and by the Pentateuch will I refute it. 'Cursed be Canaan; a servant of servants shall he be unto his brethren' (Gen. 9: 25). To whom does the property of a slave belong? To his master. Even though the land belonged to ye, through your servitude it became Israel's."

"Answer him," said the ruler.

The accusers asked for three days' time to prepare their reply, but at the end of the three days they had vanished.

Then came the Egyptians, saying, " 'God gave the Israelites favor in the eyes of the Egyptians, and they lent them gold and silver.' Now return us the gold and silver which our ancestors lent ye."

Again Gebiah appeared for the sages of Israel.

"Four hundred and thirty years," said he, "did the children of Israel dwell in Egypt. Come, now, pay us the wages of six hundred thousand men who worked for ye for naught, and we will return the gold and silver."

Then came the children of Ishmael and Ketura, before Alexander of Mukdon, saying, "The land of Canaan is ours, as it is written, 'These are the generations of Ishmael, the son of Abraham'; even as it is written, 'These are the generations of Isaac, the son of Abraham.' One son is equal to the other; come, give us our share."

Again Gebiah appeared as counsel for the sages.

"From the Pentateuch, which is your proof, will I confound ye," said he. "Is it not written, 'Abraham gave all that he had to Isaac, but unto the sons of the concubines that Abraham had, Abraham gave gifts.' The man who gives his children their inheritance during his life does not design to give it to them again after his death. To Isaac Abraham left all that he had; to his other children he gave gifts, and sent them away."

Truly a good man, say the Rabbis, was King Munmaz, a descendant of the Hashmonites. During a period of famine he gave to the poor the contents of his treasury and the treasury of his father.

His relative upbraided him for his liberality. "What thy father saved," they exclaimed, "thou hast thrown away."

Then answered Munmaz:

"My father laid up treasure here on earth; I gather it in the heavens above. 'The truth comes forth from the earth, but beneficence looks down from heaven.' My father hoarded it where hands might have been stretched forth for it; I have placed it beyond the reach of human hands. 'Thy throne is established in justice and beneficence.' For my father it produced no fruit, but for me it is bringing forth many fold. 'Say to the righteous it is good; the fruit of their labor they may eat.' My father saved money; I saved life. 'The fruit of the righteous is the tree of life. Who saves lives is a wise man.' My father saved for others; I save for myself; my father saved for this world, but I save for the next. 'Thy beneficence will go before thee; the glory of the Lord will gather thee.'

PROVERBS AND SAYINGS
OF THE RABBIS

Woe to the children banished from their father's table.

A handful of food will not satisfy the lion, neither can a pit be filled again with its own dust.

Pray to God for mercy until the last shovelful of earth is cast upon thy grave.

Cease not to pray even when the knife is laid upon thy neck.

Open not thy mouth to speak evil.

To be patient is sometimes better than to have much wealth.

The horse fed too liberally with oats becomes unruly.

Happy the pupil whose teacher approves his words.

When the cucumbers are young we may tell whether they will become good for food.

Do not to others what you would not have others do to you.

The ass complains of the cold even in July (Tamuz).

First learn and then teach.

Few are they who see their own faults.

A single light answers as well for a hundred men as for one.

Victuals prepared by many cooks will be neither hot nor cold.

The world is a wedding.

Youth is a wreath of roses.

A myrtle even in the desert remains a myrtle.

Teach thy tongue to say, "I do not know."

The house which opens not to the poor will open to the physician.

The birds of the air despise a miser.

Hospitality is an expression of Divine worship.

Thy friend has a friend, and thy friend's friend has a friend; be discreet.

Do not place a blemish on thine own flesh.

Attend no auctions if thou hast no money.

Rather skin a carcass for pay, in the public streets, than lie idly dependent on charity.

Deal with those who are fortunate.

What is intended for thy neighbor will never be thine.

The weakness of thy walls invites the burglar.

The place honors not the man, 'tis the man who gives honor to the place.

The humblest man is ruler in his own house.

If the fox is king bow before him.

If a word spoken in its time is worth one piece of money, silence in *its* time is worth two.

Tobias committed the sins and his neighbor received the punishment.

Poverty sits as gracefully upon some people as a red saddle upon a white horse.

Drain not the waters of thy well while other people may desire them.

The doctor who prescribes gratuitously gives a worthless prescription.

The rose grows among thorns.

The wine belongs to the master, but the waiter receives the thanks.

He who mixes with unclean things becomes unclean himself; he whose associations are pure becomes more holy with each day.

No man is impatient with his creditors.

Make but one sale, and thou art called a merchant.

Mention not a blemish which is thy own, in detraction of thy neighbor.

If certain goods sell not in one city, try another place.

He who reads the letter should execute the message.

A vessel used for holy purposes should not be put to uses less sacred.

Ornament thyself first, then magnify others.

Two pieces of coin in one bag make more noise than a hundred.

Man sees the mote in his neighbor's eye, but knows not of the beam in his own.

The rivalry of scholars advances science.

If thou tellest thy secret to three persons, ten know of it.

When love is intense both find room enough upon one board of the bench; afterwards they may find themselves cramped in a space of sixty cubits.

When wine enters the head the secret flies out.

When a liar speaks the truth he finds his punishment in the general disbelief.

The camel desired horns, and his ears were taken from him.

Sorrow for those who disappear never to be found.

The officer of the king is also a recipient of honors.

He who studies cannot follow a commercial life; neither can the merchant devote his time to study.

There is no occasion to light thy lamp at noontide.

Let the fruit pray for the welfare of the leaf.

Meat without salt is fit only for the dogs.

Trust not thyself until the day of thy death.

Woe to the country which hath lost its leader; woe to the ship when its captain is no more.

He who increaseth his flesh but multiplieth food for the worms.

The day is short, the labor great, and the workman slothful.

Be yielding to thy superior; be affable towards the young; be friendly with all mankind.

Silence is the fence round wisdom.

Without law, civilization perishes.

Every man will surely have his hour.

Rather be the tail among lions than the head among foxes.

Into the well which supplies thee with water cast no stones.

Many a colt's skin is fashioned to the saddle which its mother bears.

Truth is heavy, therefore few care to carry it.

Say little and do much.

He who multiplieth words will likely come to sin.

Sacrifice thy will for others, that they may be disposed to sacrifice their wills for thee.

Study today, delay not.

Look not upon thy prayers as on a task; let thy supplications be sincere.

He who is loved by man is loved by God.

Honor the sons of the poor; they give to science its splendor.

Do not live near a pious fool.

A small coin in a large jar makes a great noise.

Use thy noble vase today; tomorrow it may break.

The cat and the rat make peace over a carcass.

He who walks each day over his estate finds a coin daily.

The dog follows thee for the crumbs in thy pocket.

The soldiers fight, and the kings are heroes.

When the ox is down many are the butchers.

Descend a step in choosing thy wife; ascend a step in choosing thy friend.

Beat the gods and their priests will tremble.

The sun will set without thy assistance.

Hold no man responsible for his utterances in times of grief.

One man eats, another says grace.

He who curbs his wrath merits forgiveness for his sins.

Commit a sin twice and it will not seem to thee a crime.

While our love was strong we lay on the edge of a sword, now a couch sixty yards wide is too narrow for us.

Study is more meritorious than sacrifice.

Jerusalem was destroyed because the instruction of the young was neglected.

The world is saved by the breath of school children. Even to rebuild the Temple, the schools must not be closed.

Blessed is the son who has studied with his father, and blessed the father who has instructed his son.

Avoid wrath and thou wilt avoid sin; avoid intemperance and thou wilt not provoke Providence.

When others gather, do thou disperse; when others disperse, gather.

When thou art the only purchaser, then buy; when other buyers are present, be thou nobody.

The foolish man knows not an insult, neither does a dead man feel the cutting of a knife.

The cock and the owl both await daylight. "The light," says the cock, "brings me delight; but what in the world art thou waiting for?"

The thief who finds no opportunity to steal, considers himself an honest man.

A Galilean said, "When the shepherd is angry with his flock, he appoints for its leader a blind bellwether."

Though it is not incumbent upon thee to complete the work, thou must not therefore cease from pursuing it. If the work is great, great will be thy reward, and thy Master is faithful in His payments.

There are three crowns: of the law, the priesthood, and the kingship; but the crown of a good name is greater than them all.

Who gains wisdom? He who is willing to receive instruction from all sources. Who is the mighty man? He who subdueth his temper. Who is rich? He who is content with his lot. Who is deserving of honor? He who honoreth mankind.

Despise no man and deem nothing impossible; every man hath his hour and every thing its place.

Iron breaks stone; fire melts iron; water extinguishes fire; the clouds consume water; the storm dispels clouds; man withstands the storm; fear conquers man; wine banishes fear; sleep overcomes wine, and death is the master of sleep; but "charity," says Solomon, "saves even from death."

How canst thou escape sin? Think of three things: whence thou comest, whither thou goest, and before whom thou must appear. The scoffer, the liar, the hypocrite, and the slanderer can have no share in the future world of bliss. To slander is to commit murder.

Repent the day before thy death.*

Ten measures of wisdom came into the world; the law of Israel received nine measures, and the balance of the world one. Ten measures of beauty came into the world; Jerusalem received nine measures, and the rest of the world one.

Rabbi Simon said:

"The world stands on three pillars: law, worship, and charity."

Rabbi Ada said:

"When he who attends the synagogue regularly is prevented from being present, God asks for him."

Rabbi Simon, the son of Joshua, said:

* The Rabbi who said, "Repent the day before thy death," was asked by his disciples how they could follow his advice, as man was unable to tell upon what day his death would occur. He answered, "Consider *every* day thy last; be ever ready with penitence and good deeds."

"His enemies will humble themselves before the one who builds a place of worship."

Rabbi Lakish said:

"He who is able to attend synagogue, and neglects to do so, is a bad neighbor."

Rabbi José said:

"One need not stand upon a high place to pray, for it is written, 'Out of the depths have I called unto Thee, oh Lord'" (Ps. 30: 1). The same Rabbi prohibits moving about or talking during the progress of prayers, enlarging on Solomon's advice, "Keep thy foot when thou goest into the house of the Lord, and be more ready to hear than to offer the sacrifice of fools" (Eccl. 5: 1).

Rabbi Chia, the son of Abba, said:

"To pray loudly is not a necessity of devotion; when we pray we must direct our hearts towards heaven."

When our ancestors in the wilderness were saved from death by gazing upon the brazen serpent, it was not the serpent which killed or preserved. It was the trustful appeal to the Father in heaven.

Say the Rabbis, "Praise the Lord for the evil as for the good"; and David is given as an example when he said, "I had met with distress and sorrow, I then called on the name of the Lord" (Ps. 116).

Rabbi Ashi said:

"Charity is greater than all."

Rabbi Eliazar said:

"Who gives charity in secret is greater than Moses."

He finds authority for this saying in the words of Moses (Deut. 9: 19), "For I was afraid of the anger," and the words of Solomon (Prov. 21: 14), which he presents as an answer, "A gift given in secret pacifieth anger."

Rabbi Joshua said:

"A miser is as wicked as an idolater."

Rabbi Eliazar said:

"Charity is more than sacrifices."

Rabbi Jochanan said:

"He who gives (charity) becomes rich," or as it is written, "A beneficent soul will be abundantly gratified."

One day a philosopher inquired of Rabbi Akiba, "If your God loves the poor, why does He not support them?"

"God allows the poor to be with us ever," responded Akiba, "that the opportunities for doing good may never fail."

"But," returned the philosopher, "how do you know that this virtue of charity pleases God? If a master punishes his slaves by depriving them of food and clothing, does he feel pleased when others feed and clothe them?"

"But suppose, on the other hand," said the Rabbi, "that the children of a tender father, children whom he could no longer justly assist, had fallen into poverty, would he be displeased if kind souls pitied and aided them? We are not the slaves of a hard master. God calls us His children, and Himself we call our Father."

Rabbah said:

"When one stands at the judgment-seat of God these questions are asked:

" 'Hast thou been honest in all thy dealings?'

" 'Hast thou set aside a portion of thy time for the study of the law?'

" 'Hast thou observed the first commandment?'

" 'Hast thou, in trouble, still hoped and believed in God?'

" 'Hast thou spoken wisely?' "

"All the blessings of a household come through the wife, therefore should her husband honor her."

Rab said:

"Men should be careful lest they cause women to weep, for God counts their tears.

"In cases of charity, where both men and women claim relief, the latter should be first assisted. If there should not be enough for both, the men should cheerfully relinquish their claims.

"A woman's death is felt by nobody as by her husband.

"Tears are shed on God's altar for the one who forsakes his first love.

"He who loves his wife as himself, and honors her more than himself, will train his children properly; he will meet, too, the fulfilment of the verse, 'And thou shalt know that there is peace in thy tent, and thou wilt look over thy habitation and shall miss nothing'" (Job 5: 24).

Rabbi José said:

"I never call my wife 'wife,' but 'home,' for she, indeed, makes my home.

"He who possesses a knowledge of God, and a knowledge of man, will not easily commit sin.

"The Bible was given us to establish peace.

"He who wrongs his fellow-man, even in so small a coin as a penny, is as wicked as if he should take life.

"He who raises his hand against his fellow in passion is a sinner.

"Be not the friend of one who wears the cloak of a saint to cover the deformities of a fool."

Rabbi Simon said:

"One who gives way to passion is as bad as an idolater.

"Hospitality is as great a virtue as studying the law."

"Never put thyself in the way of temptation," advised Rabbi Judah; "even David could not resist it."

Rabbi Tyra, on being asked by his pupils to tell them the secret which had gained him a happy, peaceful old age, replied, "I have never cherished anger with my family; I have never envied those greater than myself, and I have never rejoiced in the downfall of any one."

"Unhappy is he who mistakes the branch for the tree, the shadow for the substance.

"Thy yesterday is thy past; thy today thy future; thy tomorrow is a secret.

"The best preacher is the heart; the best teacher is time; the best book is the world; the best friend is God.

"Life is but a loan to man; death is the creditor who will one day claim it.

"Understand a man by his own deeds and words. The impressions of others lead to false judgment."

Rabbi Jacob said:

"He through whose agency another has been falsely punished stands outside of heaven's gates."

Rabbi Isaac said:

"The sins of the bad-tempered are greater than his merits."

Rabbi Lakish said:

"The man who sins is foolish as well as wicked."

Rabbi Samuel said:

"The good actions which we perform in this world take form and meet us in the world to come.

"Better to bear a false accusation in silence, than by speaking to bring the guilty to public shame.

"He who can feel ashamed will not readily do wrong.

"There is a great difference between one who can feel ashamed before his own soul and one who is only ashamed before his fellow-man."

Rabbi Akiba said:

"God's covenant with us included work; for the command, 'Six days shalt thou work and the seventh shalt thou rest,' made the 'rest' conditional upon the 'work.'"

Rabbi Simon said, on the same subject:

"God first told Adam to dress the Garden of Eden, and to keep it (Gen. 2: 15), and then permitted him to eat of the fruit of his labor."

Rabbi Tarphon said:

"God did not dwell in the midst of Israel till they had worked to deserve His presence, for he commanded, 'They shall make me a sanctuary, and then I will dwell in the midst of them.'"

When Jerusalem was in the hands of the Romans, one of their philosophers asked of the Rabbis:

"If your God dislikes idolatry, why does He not destroy the idols and so put temptation out of the way?"

The wise men answered:

"Would you have the sun and the moon destroyed because of the foolish ones who worship them? To change the course of nature to punish sinners, would bring suffering to the innocent also."

In Ecclesiastes 9: 14, we find this verse:

"There was a little city and the men therein were few, and there came against it a great king, and built around it great works of siege; but there was found in it a poor wise man, and he delivered the city by his wisdom."

The sages interpret this verse most beautifully. The "little city" is man, and the "few men" are his different qualities. The "king" who besieged it is evil inclination, and the "great bulwarks" he built around it are "evil deeds." The "poor wise man" who saved the city is the "good actions" which the poorest may readily perform.

Rabbi Judah said:

"He who refuses to teach a precept to his pupil is guilty of theft, just as one who steals from the inheritance of his father; as it is written, 'The law which Moses commanded us is the inheritance of the congregation of Jacob.' (Deut.) But if he teaches him, what is his reward?"

Raba says, "He will obtain the blessing of Joseph."

Rabbi Eleazer said:

"That house where the law is not studied by night should be destroyed.

"The wealthy man who aids not the scholar desirous of studying God's law will not prosper.

"He who changes his word, saying one thing and doing another, is even as he who serveth idols."

Rabbi Chamah, the son of Papa, said:

"He who eats or drinks and blesses not the Lord, is even as he who stealeth, for it is said, 'The heavens are the heavens of the Lord, and the earth hath He given to the children of men.' "

Rabbi Simon, the son of Lakish, said:

"They who perform one precept in this world will find it recorded for their benefit in the world to come; as it is written, 'Thy righteousness will go before thee, the glory of the Lord will gather thee in.' And the same will be the case, in contrast, with those who sin. For the Bible says, 'Which I commanded thee this day to do them,' to 'do them,' the precepts, today, though the reward is not promised today; but in the future, ordinances obeyed, will testify in thy favor, for 'thy righteousness will go before thee.' "

The Rabbis pronounced those the "friends of God," who being offended thought not of revenge; who practiced good through love for God, and who were cheerful under suffering and difficulties. Of such Isaiah wrote, "They shall shine forth like the sun at noonday."

Love thy wife as thyself; honor her more than thyself. He who lives unmarried, lives without joy. If thy wife is small, bend down to her and whisper in her ear. He who sees his wife die, has, as it were, been present at the destruction of the sanctuary itself. The children of a man who marries for money will prove a curse to him.

He who has more learning than good deeds is like a tree with many branches but weak roots; the first great storm will throw it to the ground. He whose good works are greater than his knowledge is like a tree with fewer branches but with strong and spreading roots, a tree which all the winds of heaven cannot uproot.

Better is the curse of the righteous man than the blessing of the wicked. Better the curse of Achia, the Shelonite, than the blessing of Bil'am, the son of Beor. Thus did Achia curse the Israelites, "And the Lord will smite Israel as the reed is shaken in the water" (Kings 14: 15). The reed bends but it breaks not, for it groweth by the water, and its roots are strong. Thus did Bil'am bless Israel, "As cedar trees beside the waters." Cedars do not grow beside the waters; their roots are weak, and when strong winds blow they break in pieces.

LEGENDS

The Desert Island

A very wealthy man, who was of a kind, benevolent disposition, desired to make his slave happy. He gave him, therefore, his freedom, and presented him with a shipload of merchandise.

"Go," said he, "sail to different countries, dispose of these goods, and that which thou mayest receive for them shall be thy own."

The slave sailed away upon the broad ocean, but before he had been long upon his voyage a storm overtook him; his ship was driven on a rock and went to pieces; all on board were lost, all save this slave, who swam to an island shore near by. Sad, despondent, with naught in the world, he traversed this island, until he approached a large and beautiful city; and many people approached him joyously, shouting, "Welcome! welcome! Long live the king!" They brought a rich carriage, and placing him therein, escorted him to a magnificent palace, where many servants gathered about him, clothing him in royal garments, addressing him as their sovereign, and expressing their obedience to his will.

The slave was amazed and dazzled, believing that he was dreaming, and all that he saw, heard, and experienced was mere passing fantasy. Becoming convinced of the reality of his condition, he said to some men about him for whom he experienced a friendly feeling:

"How is this? I cannot understand it. That you should thus elevate and honor a man whom you know not, a poor, naked wanderer, whom you have never seen before, making him your ruler, causes me more wonder than I can readily express."

"Sire," they replied, "this island is inhabited by spirits. Long since they prayed to God to send them yearly a son of man to reign over them, and He has answered their prayers. Yearly he sends them a son of man, whom they receive with honor and elevate to the throne; but his dignity and power ends with the year. With its close his royal garments are taken from him, he is placed on board a ship and carried to a vast and desolate island, where, unless he has previously been wise and prepared for this day, he will find neither friend nor subject, and be obliged to pass a weary, lonely, miserable life. Then a new king is selected here, and so year follows year. The kings who preceded thee were careless and indifferent, enjoying their power to the full, and thinking not of the day when it should end. Be wiser thou; let our words find rest within thy heart."

The newly-made king listened attentively to all this, and felt grieved that he should have lost even the time he had already missed for making preparations for his loss of power.

He addressed the wise man who had spoken, saying, "Advise me, oh, spirit of wisdom, how I may prepare for the days which will come upon me in the future."

"Naked thou camest to us and naked thou wilt be sent to the desolate island of which I have told thee," replied the other. "At present thou art king, and may do as pleaseth thee; therefore send workmen to this island; let them build houses, till the ground, and beautify the surroundings. The barren soil will be changed into fruitful fields, people will journey there to live, and thou wilt have established a new kingdom for thyself, with subjects to welcome thee in gladness when thou shalt have lost

thy power here. The year is short, the work is long; therefore be earnest and energetic."

The king followed this advice. He sent workmen and
materials to the desolate island, and before the close of
his temporary power it had become a blooming, pleasant,
and attractive spot. The rulers who had preceded him had
anticipated the day of their power's close with dread, or
smothered all thought of it in revelry; but he looked forward to it as a day of joy, when he should enter upon a
career of permanent peace and happiness.

The day came; the freed slave, who had been made
king, was deprived of his authority; with his power he lost
his royal garments; naked he was placed upon a ship, and
its sails set for the desolate isle.

When he approached its shores, however, the people
whom he had sent there came to meet him with music,
song, and great joy. They made him a prince among them,
and he lived with them ever after in pleasantness and
peace.

The wealthy man of kindly disposition is God, and the
slave to whom He gave freedom is the soul which He
gives to man. The island at which the slave arrives is the
world; naked and weeping he appears to his parents, who
are the inhabitants that greet him warmly and make him
their king. The friends who tell him of the ways of the
country are his "good inclinations." The year of his reign
is his span of life, and the desolate island is the future
world, which he must beautify by good deeds, "the workmen and material," or else live lonely and desolate for
ever.

The Emperor and the Aged Man

The Emperor Adrian, passing through the streets of
Tiberias, noticed a very old man planting a fig tree, and
pausing, said to him:

"Wherefore plant that tree? If thou didst labor in thy youth, thou shouldst now have a store for thy old age, and surely of the fruit of this tree thou canst not hope to eat."

The old man answered:

"In my youth I worked, and I still work. With God's good pleasure I may e'en partake of the fruit of this tree I plant. I am in His hands."

"Tell me thy age," said the emperor.

"I have lived for a hundred years."

"A hundred years old, and still expect to eat from the fruit of this tree?"

"If such be God's pleasure," replied the old man; "if not, I will leave it for my son, as my father left the fruit of his labor for me."

"Well," said the emperor, "if thou dost live until the figs from this tree are ripe, I pray thee let me know of it."

The aged man lived to partake of that very fruit, and remembering the emperor's words, he resolved to visit him. So, taking a small basket, he filled it with the choicest figs from the tree, and proceeded on his errand. Telling the palace guard his purpose, he was admitted to the sovereign's presence.

"Well," asked the emperor, "what is thy wish?"

The old man replied:

"Lo, I am the old man to whom thou didst say, on the day thou sawest him planting a fig tree, 'If thou livest to eat of its fruit, I pray thee let me know'; and behold I have come and brought thee of the fruit, that thou mayest partake of it likewise."

The emperor was very much pleased, and emptying the man's basket of its figs, he ordered it to be filled with gold coins.

When the old man had departed, the courtiers said to the emperor:

"Why didst thou so honor this old Jew?"

"The Lord hath honored him, and why not I?" replied the emperor.

Now next door to this old man there lived a woman, who, when she heard of her neighbor's good fortune, desired her husband to try his luck in the same quarter. She filled for him an immense basket with figs, and bidding him put it on his shoulder, said, "Now carry it to the emperor; he loves figs and will fill thy basket with golden coin."

When her husband approached the gates of the palace, he told his errand to the guards, saying, "I brought these figs to the emperor; empty my basket I pray, and fill it up again with gold."

When this was told to the emperor, he ordered the old man to stand in the hallway of the palace, and all who passed pelted him with his figs. He returned home wounded and crestfallen to his disappointed wife.

"Never mind, thou hast one consolation," said she; "had they been cocoanuts instead of figs thou mightest have suffered harder raps."

Proving a Claim

A citizen of Jerusalem traveling through the country was taken very sick at an inn. Feeling that he would not recover, he sent for the landlord and said to him, "I am going the way of all flesh. If after my death any party should come from Jerusalem and claim my effects, do not deliver them until he shall prove to thee by three wise acts that he is entitled to them; for I charged my son before starting upon my way, that if death befell me he would be obliged to prove his wisdom before obtaining my possessions."

The man died and was buried according to Jewish rites, and his death was made public that his heirs might appear. When his son learned of his father's decease he started from Jerusalem for the place where he had died. Near the gates of the city he met a man who had a load of wood for sale. This he purchased and ordered it to be delivered at the inn towards which he was traveling. The man from whom he bought it went at once to the inn, and said, "Here is the wood."

"What wood?" returned the proprietor; "I ordered no wood."

"No," answered the woodcutter, "but the man who follows me did; I will enter and wait for him."

Thus the son had provided for himself a welcome when he should reach the inn, which was his first wise act.

The landlord said to him, "Who art thou?"

"The son of the merchant who died in thy house," he replied.

They prepared for him a dinner, and placed upon the table five pigeons and a chicken. The master of the house, his wife, two sons, and two daughters sat with him at the table.

"Serve the food," said the landlord.

"Nay," answered the young man; "thou art master, it is thy privilege."

"I desire thee to do this thing; thou art my guest, the merchant's son; pray help the food."

The young man thus entreated divided one pigeon between the sons, another between the two daughters, gave the third to the man and his wife, and kept the other two for himself. This was his second wise act.

The landlord looked somewhat perplexed at this mode of distribution, but said nothing.

Then the merchant's son divided the chicken. He gave to the landlord and his wife the head, to the two sons the legs, to the two daughters the wings, and took the body for himself. This was his third wise act.

The landlord said:

"Is this the way they do things in thy country? I noticed the manner in which thou didst apportion the pigeons, but said nothing; but the chicken, my dear sir! I must really ask thee thy meaning."

Then the young man answered:

"I told thee that it was not my place to serve the food, nevertheless when thou didst insist I did the best I could, and I think I have succeeded. Thyself, thy wife, and one pigeon make three; thy two sons and one pigeon make three; thy two daughters and one pigeon make three; and myself and two pigeons make three also, therefore is it fairly done. As regards the chicken, I gave to thee and thy wife the head, because ye are the heads of the family; I gave to each of thy sons a leg, because they are the pillars of the family, preserving always the family name; I gave to each of thy daughters a wing, because in the natural course of events they will marry, take wing, and fly away from the home-nest. I took the body of the chicken because it looks like a ship, and in a ship I came here and in a ship I hope to return. I am the son of the merchant who died in thy house; give me the property of my dead father."

"Take it and go," said the landlord. And giving him his father's possessions the young man departed in peace.

A Payment with Interest

A certain man, a native of Athina (a city near Jerusalem), visited the city of Jerusalem, and after leaving it, ridiculed the place and its inhabitants. The Jerusalemites were very wroth at being made the subjects of his sport, and they induced one of their citizens to travel to Athina, to induce the man to return to Jerusalem, which would give them an opportunity to punish his insolence.

The citizen thus commissioned reached Athina, and

very shortly fell in with the man whom he had come to meet. Walking through the streets together one day, the man from Jerusalem said, "See, the string of my shoe is broken; take me, I pray, to the shoemaker."

The shoemaker repaired the string, and the man paid him a coin more in value than the worth of the shoes.

Next day, when walking with the same man, he broke the string of his other shoe, and going to the shoemaker, he paid him the same large sum for repairing that.

"Why," said the man of Athina, "shoes must be very dear in Jerusalem, when thou payest such a price but for repairing a string."

"Yes," answered the other; "they bring nine ducats, and even in the cheapest times from seven to eight."

"Then it would be a profitable employment for me to take shoes from my city and sell them in thine."

"Yes, indeed; and if thou wilt but let me know of thy coming I will put thee in the way of customers."

So the man of Athina, who had made merry over the Jerusalemites, bought a large stock of shoes and set out for Jerusalem, informing his friend of his coming. The latter started to meet him, and greeting him before he came to the gates of the city, said to him:

"Before a stranger may enter and sell goods in Jerusalem, he must shave his head and blacken his face. Art thou ready to do this?"

"And why not," replied the other, "as long as I have a prospect of large profits; why should I falter or hesitate at so slight a thing as that?"

So the stranger, shaving the hair from his head and blackening his face (by which all Jerusalem knew him as the man who had ridiculed the city), took up his place in the market, with his wares spread before him.

Buyers paused before his stall, and asked him:

"How much for the shoes?"

"Ten ducats a pair," he answered; "or I may sell for nine; but certainly for not less than eight."

This caused a great laugh and uproar in the market, and the stranger was driven from it in derision and his shoes thrown after him.

Seeking the Jerusalemite who had deceived him, he said:

"Why hast thou so treated me? did I so to thee in Athina?"

"Let this be a lesson to thee," answered the Jerusalemite. "I do not think thou wilt be so ready to make sport of us in the future."

The Weasel and the Well

A young man, upon his journeys through the country, fell in with a young woman, and they became mutually attached. When the young man was obliged to leave the neighborhood of the damsel's residence, they met to say "goodby." During the parting they pledged a mutual faith, and each promised to wait until, in the course of time, they might be able to marry. "Who will be the witness of our betrothal?" said the young man. Just then they saw a weasel run past them and disappear in the wood. "See," he continued, "this weasel and this well of water by which we are standing shall be the witnesses of our betrothal"; and so they parted. Years passed, the maiden remained true, but the youth married. A son was born to him, and grew up the delight of his parents. One day while the child was playing he became tired, and lying upon the ground fell asleep. A weasel bit him in the neck, and he bled to death. The parents were consumed with grief by this calamity, and it was not until another son was given them that they forgot their sorrow. But when this second child was able to walk alone it wandered without the house, and bending over the well, looking at its shadow in the water, lost its balance and was drowned. Then the father recollected his perjured vow, and his witnesses, the weasel and the well. He told his wife of the circumstance, and she agreed to a divorce. He then sought the maiden to whom he had promised marriage, and found her still awaiting his return. He told her how, through God's agency, he had been punished for his wrongdoing, after which they married and lived in peace.

The Lawful Heir

A wise Israelite, dwelling some distance from Jerusalem, sent his son to the Holy City to complete his education. During his son's absence the father was taken ill, and feeling that death was upon him he made a will, leaving all his property to one of his slaves, on condition that he should allow the son to select any one article which pleased him for an inheritance.

As soon as his master died, the slave, elated with his good fortune, hastened to Jerusalem, informed his late master's son of what had taken place, and showed him the will.

The young man was surprised and grieved at the intelligence, and after the allotted time of mourning had expired, he began to seriously consider his situation. He went to his teacher, explained the circumstances to him, read him his father's will, and expressed himself bitterly on account of the disappointment of his reasonable hopes and expectations. He could think of nothing that he had done to offend his father, and was loud in his complaints of injustice.

"Stop," said his teacher; "thy father was a man of wisdom and a loving relative. This will is a living monument to his good sense and far-sightedness. May his son prove as wise in his day."

"What!" exclaimed the young man. "I see no wisdom in his bestowal of his property upon a slave; no affection in this slight upon his only son."

"Listen," returned the teacher. "By his action thy father hath but secured thy inheritance to thee, if thou art wise enough to avail thyself of his understanding. Thus thought he when he felt the hand of death approaching, 'My son is away; when I am dead he will not be here to take charge of my affairs; my slaves will plunder my estate, and to gain time will even conceal my death from my son, and deprive me of the sweet savor of mourning.' To prevent these things he bequeathed his property to his slave, well knowing that the slave, believing in his apparent right, would give thee speedy information and take care of the effects, even as he has done."

"Well, well, and how does this benefit me?" impatiently interrupted the pupil.

"Ah!" replied the teacher, "wisdom I see rests not with the young. Dost thou not know that what a slave possesses belongs but to his master? Has not thy father left thee the right to select one article of all his property for thy own? Choose the slave as thy portion, and by possessing him thou wilt recover all that was thy father's. Such was his wise and loving intention."

The young man did as he was advised, and gave the slave his freedom afterwards. But ever after he was wont to exclaim:

"Wisdom resides with the aged, and understanding in length of days."

Nothing in the World without its Use

David, King of Israel, was once lying upon his couch and many thoughts were passing through his mind.

"Of what use in this world is the spider?" thought he;

"it but increases the dust and dirt of the world, making places unsightly and causing great annoyance."

Then he thought of an insane man:

"How unfortunate is such a being. I know that all things are ordained by God with reason and purpose, yet this is beyond my comprehension; why should men be born idiots, or grow insane?"

Then the mosquitoes annoyed him, and the king thought:

"What can the mosquito be good for? why was it created in the world? It but disturbs our comfort, and the world profits not by its existence."

Yet King David lived to discover that these very insects, and the very condition of life, the being of which he deplored, were ordained even to his own benefit.

When he fled from before Saul, David was captured in the land of the Philistines by the brothers of Goliath, who carried him before the king of Gath, and it was only by pretending idiocy that he escaped death, the king deeming it impossible that such a man could be the kingly David; as it is written, "And he disguised his reason before their eyes, and played the madman in their hands, and scribbled on the doors of the gate, and let his spittle run down upon his beard" (Sam. 21: 12-16).

Upon another occasion David hid himself in the cave of Adullam, and after he had entered the cave it chanced that a spider spun a web over the opening thereto. His pursuers passed that way, but thinking that no one could have entered the cave protected by the spider's web without destroying it, they continued on their way.

The mosquito also was of service to David when he entered the camp of Saul to secure the latter's weapon. While stooping near Abner, the sleeping man moved and placed his leg upon David's body. If he moved, he would awake Abner and meet with death, if he remained in that position morning would dawn and bring him death; he knew not what to do, when a mosquito alighted upon Abner's leg; he moved it quickly, and David escaped.

Therefore sang David:

"All my bones shall say, O Lord, who is like unto Thee."

The Reward of Faith

The Israelites were commanded to visit Jerusalem on three festivals. It happened upon one occasion that there was a scarcity of water in the city. One of the people called upon a certain nobleman who was the owner of three wells, and asked him for the use of the water which they contained, promising that they should be refilled by a stated date, and contracting in default of this to pay a certain large amount in silver as forfeit. The day came, there had been no rain, and the three wells were dry. In the morning the owner of the wells sent for the promised money. Nakdemon, the son of Gurion, the man who had undertaken this burden for his people's sake, replied, "The day is but begun; there is yet time."

He entered the Temple and prayed that God might send rain and save him all his fortune which he had ventured. His prayer was answered. The clouds gathered and the rain fell. As he passed out of the Temple with a grateful heart, he was met by his creditor, who said:

"True, the rain has refilled my wells, but it is dark; the day has gone, and according to our agreement thou must still pay me the promised sum."

Once more Nakdemon prayed, and lo, the clouds lifted and the sinking sun smiled brightly on the spot where the men stood, showing that the sunlight of day was still there, though the rain-clouds had temporarily obscured its gleams.

Abtinoss and Garmah

There was a certain family, the family of Abtinoss, the members of which were learned in the art of preparing the incense used in the service. Their knowledge they refused to impart to others, and the directors of the Temple, fearing that the art might die with them, discharged them from the service, and brought other parties from Alexandria, in Egypt, to prepare the sweet perfume. These latter were unable to afford satisfaction, however, and the directors were obliged to give the service back into the hands of the family of Abtinoss, who on their part refused to accept it again, unless the remuneration for their services was doubled. When asked why they so persistently refused to impart their skill to others, they replied that they feared they might teach some unworthy persons, who would afterwards use their knowledge in an idolatrous worship. The members of this family were very particular not to use perfume of any kind themselves, lest the people should imagine that they put the sweet spices used in the manufacture of the incense to a baser use.

An exactly similar case to the above occurred with the family of Garmah, which had the monopoly of the knowledge of preparing the show-bread used in the services of the Temple.

It was in reference to these cases that the son of Azai said, "In thy name they shall call thee, and in thy city they shall cause thee to live, and from thy own they will give thee," meaning that trustful persons should not fear that others might steal their occupations; "for in thy name they will call thee," as with the families of Abtinoss and Garmah; "and from thy own they will give thee," meaning that what a man earns is his own, and cannot be taken away.

Trust in God

Rabbi Jochanan, the son of Levi, fasted and prayed to the Lord that he might be permitted to gaze on the angel Elijah, he who had ascended alive to heaven. God granted his prayer, and in the semblance of a man Elijah appeared before him.

"Let me journey with thee in thy travels through the world," prayed the Rabbi to Elijah; "let me observe thy doings, and gain in wisdom and understanding."

"Nay," answered Elijah; "my actions thou couldst not understand; my doings would trouble thee, being beyond thy comprehension."

But still the Rabbi entreated:

"I will neither trouble nor question thee," he said; "only let me accompany thee on thy way."

"Come, then," said Elijah; "but let thy tongue be mute. With thy first question, thy first expression of astonishment, we must part company."

So the two journeyed through the world together. They approached the house of a poor man, whose only treasure and means of support was a cow. As they came near, the man and his wife hastened to meet them, begged them to enter their cot, and eat and drink of the best they could afford, and to pass the night under their roof. This they did, receiving every attention from their poor but hospitable host and hostess. In the morning Elijah rose up early and prayed to God, and when he had finished his prayer, behold the cow belonging to the poor people dropped dead. Then the travelers continued on their journey.

Much was Rabbi Jochanan perplexed. "Not only did we neglect to pay them for their hospitality and generous services, but his cow we have killed"; and he said to Elijah, "Why didst thou kill the cow of this good man, who——"

"Peace," interrupted Elijah; "hear, see, and be silent! If I answer thy questions we must part."

And they continued on their way together.

Towards evening they arrived at a large and imposing mansion, the residence of a haughty and wealthy man. They were coldly received; a piece of bread and a glass of water were placed before them, but the master of the house did not welcome or speak to them, and they remained there during the night unnoticed. In the morning Elijah remarked that a wall of the house required repairing, and sending for a carpenter, he himself paid the money for the repair, as a return, he said, for the hospitality they had received.

Again was Rabbi Jochanan filled with wonder, but he said naught, and they proceeded on their journey.

As the shades of night were falling they entered a city which contained a large and imposing synagogue. As it was the time of the evening service they entered and were much pleased with the rich adornments, the velvet cushions, and gilded carvings of the interior. After the completion of the service, Elijah arose and called out aloud, "Who is here willing to feed and lodge two poor men this night?" none answered, and no respect was shown to the traveling strangers. In the morning, however, Elijah reentered the synagogue, and shaking its members by the hands, he said, "I hope that you may all become presidents."

Next evening the two entered another city, when the *Shamas* (sexton) of the synagogue, came to meet them, and notifying the members of his congregation of the coming of two strangers, the best hotel of the place was opened to them, and all vied in showing them attention and honor.

In the morning, on parting with them, Elijah said, "May the Lord appoint over you but one president."

Jochanan could resist his curiosity no longer. "Tell me,"

said he to Elijah, "tell me the meaning of all these actions which I have witnessed. To those who have treated us coldly thou hast uttered good wishes; to those who have been gracious to us thou hast made no suitable return. Even though we must part, I pray thee explain to me the meaning of thy acts."

"Listen," said Elijah, "and learn to trust in God, even though thou canst not understand His ways. We first entered the house of the poor man, who treated us so kindly. Know that it had been decreed that on that very day his wife should die. I prayed unto the Lord that the cow might prove a redemption for her; God granted my prayers, and the woman was preserved unto her husband. The rich man, whom next we called up, treated us coldly, and I repaired his wall. I repaired it without a new foundation, without digging to the old one. Had he repaired it himself he would have dug, and thus discovered a treasure which lies there buried, but which is now for ever lost to him. To the members of the synagogue who were inhospitable I said, 'May you all be presidents,' and where many rule there can be no peace; but to the others I said, 'May you have but one president'; with one leader no misunderstanding may arise. Now, if thou seest the wicked prospering, be not envious; if thou seest the righteous in poverty and trouble, be not provoked or doubtful of God's justice. The Lord is righteous, His judgments all are true; His eyes note all mankind, and none can say, 'What dost thou?' "

With these words Elijah disappeared, and Jochanan was left alone.

The Bride and Bridegroom

There was once a man who pledged his dearest faith to a maiden, beautiful and true. For a time all passed pleasantly, and the maiden lived in happiness. But then the man was called from her side, he left her; long she waited, but he did not return. Friends pitied her and rivals mocked her; tauntingly they pointed at her, and said, "He has left thee; he will never come back." The maiden sought her chamber, and read in secret the letters which her lover had written to her, the letters in which he promised to be ever faithful, ever true. Weeping she read them, but they brought comfort to her heart; she dried her eyes and doubted not.

A joyous day dawned for her; the man she loved returned, and when he learned that others had doubted and asked her how she had preserved her faith, she showed his letters to him, declaring her eternal trust.

Israel, in misery and captivity, was mocked by the nations; her hopes of redemption were made a laughing-stock; her sages scoffed at; her holy men derided. Into her synagogues, into her schools went Israel; she read the letters which her God had written, and believed in the holy promises which they contained.

God will in time redeem her; and when He says:

"How could you alone be faithful of all the mocking nations?"

She will point to the law and answer:

"Had not Thy law been my delight, I should long since have perished in my affliction" (Psalm 119).

Truth

When God was about to create man the angels gathered about him. Some of them opening their lips exclaimed, "Create, oh God, a being who shall praise Thee from earth even as we in heaven sing Thy glory."

But others said:

"Hear us, Almighty King, create no more! The glorious harmony of the heavens which Thou hast sent to earth will be my man disturbed, destroyed."

Then silence fell upon the contesting hosts as the Angel

of Mercy appeared before the throne of grace on bended knees.

Sweet was the voice which said entreatingly:

"Oh, Father, create Thou man; make him Thine own noble image. With heavenly pity will I fill his heart, with sympathy towards every living thing impress his being; through him will they find cause to praise Thee."

Then the Angel of Mercy ceased, and the Angel of Peace with tearful eyes spoke thus:

"O God, create him not! Thy peace he will disturb, the flow of blood will follow sure his coming. Confusion, horror, war, will blot the earth, and Thou wilt no longer find a pleasant place among Thy works on earth."

Then spoke in stern tones the Angel of Justice:

"And Thou wilt judge him, God; he shall be subject to my sway."

The Angel of Truth approached, saying:

"Cease! Oh God of truth, with man Thou sendest falsehood to the earth."

Then all were silent, and out of the deep quietness the Divine words came:

"Thou, oh Truth, shalt go to earth with him, and yet remain a denizen of heaven; 'twixt heaven and earth to float, connecting link between the two."

The Destruction of Bithar

It was customary in Bithar when a child was born for the parents to plant a young cedar tree, to grow up with the infant. It happened upon one occasion when the daughter of the emperor was riding through the city, that her chariot broke down, and her attendants pulled up a young cedar tree to use in repairing it. The man who had planted the tree, seeing this, attacked the servants and beat them severely. This action incensed the emperor, who immediately dispatched an army of eighty thousand men against the city. These captured it and killed the inhabitants, men, women and children. The rivers ran red with blood, and 'tis said that the ground was rich and prolific to the farmers for seven years, from the bodies of those who perished, said to be four hundred thousand Israelites.

The Destruction of Jerusalem

When the guilt of the Israelites grew too great for the forbearance of the Most High, and they refused to listen to the words and warnings of Jeremiah, the prophet left Jerusalem and traveled to the land of Benjamin. While he was in the holy city, and prayed for mercy on it, it was spared; but while he sojourned in the land of Benjamin, Nebuchadnezzar laid waste the land of Israel, plundered the holy Temple, robbed it of its ornaments, and gave it a prey to the devouring flames. By the hands of Nebuzaradan did Nebuchadnezzar send (while he himself remained in Riblah) to destroy Jerusalem.

Before he ordered the expedition he endeavored by means of signs, in accordance with the superstition of his age, to ascertain the result of the attempt. He shot an arrow from his bow, pointing to the west, and the arrow turned towards Jerusalem. Then he shot again, pointing towards the east, and the arrow sped towards Jerusalem. Then he shot once more, desiring to know in which direction lay the guilty city which should be blotted from the world, and for the third time his arrow pointed towards Jerusalem.

When the city had been captured, he marched with his princes and officers into the Temple, and called out mockingly to the God of Israel, "And art thou the great God before whom the world trembles, and we here in thy city and thy Temple!"

On one of the walls he found the mark of an arrow's head, as though somebody had been killed or hit near by, and he asked, "Who was killed here?"

"Zachariah, the son of Yehoyadah, the high priest," answered the people; "he rebuked us incessantly on account of our transgressions, and we tired of his words, and put him to death."

The followers of Nebuchadnezzar massacred the inhabitants of Jerusalem, the priests and the people, old and young, women, and children who were attending school, even babies in the cradle. The feast of blood at last shocked even the leader of the hostile heathens, who ordered a stay of this wholesale murder. He then removed all the vessels of gold and silver from the Temple, and sent them by his ships, to Babel, after which he set the Temple on fire.

The high priest donned his robe and ephod, and saying, "Now that the Temple is destroyed, no priest is needed to officiate," threw himself into the flames and was consumed. When the other priests who were still alive witnessed this action, they took their harps and musical instruments and followed the example of the high priest. Those of the people whom the soldiers had not killed were bound in iron chains, burdened with the spoils of the victors, and carried into captivity. Jeremiah the prophet returned to Jerusalem and accompanied his unfortunate brethren, who went out almost naked. When they reached a place called *Bet Kuro,* Jeremiah obtained better clothing for them. And he spoke to Nebuchadnezzar and the Chaldeans, and said, "Think not that of your own strength you were able to overcome the people chosen of the Lord; 'tis their iniquities which have condemned them to this sorrow."

Thus the people journeyed on with crying and moaning until they reached the rivers of Babylon. Then Nebuchadnezzar said to them, "Sing, ye people—play for me—sing the songs ye were wont to sing before your great Lord in Jerusalem."

In answer to this command, the Levites hung their harps upon the willow trees near the banks of the river, as it is written, "Upon the willows in her midst had we hung up our harps" (Ps. 137: 2). Then they said, "If we had but performed the will of God and sung His praises devoutly, we should not have been delivered into thy hands. Now, how can we sing before thee the prayers and hymns that belong only to the One Eternal God?" as it is said, "How should we sing the song of the Lord on the soil of the stranger?" (Ibid. 4).

Then said the officers of the captors, "These men are men of death; they refuse to obey the order of the king; let them die."

But forth stepped Pelatya, the son of Yehoyadah, and thus he addressed Nebuchadnezzar:

"Behold, if a flock is delivered into the hands of a shepherd, and a wolf steals a lamb from the flock, tell me, who is responsible to the owner of the lost animal?"

"Surely the shepherd," replied Nebuchadnezzar.

"Then listen to thine own words," replied Pelatya. "God has given Israel into thy hands; to Him art thou responsible for those who are slain."

The king ordered the chains to be removed from the captives, and they were not put to death.

Second Destruction of Jerusalem

Through Kamtzah and Bar Kamtzah was Jerusalem destroyed; and thus it happened.

A certain man made a feast; he was a friend of Kamtzah, but Bar Kamtzah he hated. He sent a messenger to Kamtzah with an invitation to his banquet, but this messenger making a mistake, delivered the invitation to his master's enemy, Bar Kamtzah.

Bar Kamtzah accepted the invitation, and was on hand at the appointed time, but when the host saw his enemy enter his house, he ordered him to leave at once.

"Nay," said Bar Kamtzah, "now that I am here, do not so insult me as to send me forth. I will pay thee for all that I may eat and drink."

"I want not thy money," returned the other, "neither do I desire thy presence; get thee gone at once."

But Bar Kamtzah persisted.

"I will pay the entire expense of thy feast," he said; "do not let me be degraded in the eyes of thy guests."

The host was determined, and Bar Kamtzah withdrew from the banquet-room in anger.

"Many Rabbis were present," said he in his heart, "and not one of them interfered in my behalf, therefore this insult which they saw put upon me must have pleased them."

So Bar Kamtzah spoke treacherously of the Jews unto the king, saying, "The Jews have rebelled against thee."

"How can I know this?" inquired the king.

"Send a sacrifice to their Temple and it will be rejected," replied Bar Kamtzah.

The ruler then sent a well-conditioned calf to be sacrificed for him in the Temple, but through the machinations of Bar Kamtzah the messenger inflicted a blemish upon it, and, of course, not being fit for the sacrifice (Lev. 22: 21) it was not accepted.

Through this cause was Cæsar sent to capture Jerusalem, and for two years he besieged the city. Four wealthy citizens of Jerusalem had stored up enough food to last the inhabitants a much longer time than this, but the people being anxious to fight with the Romans, destroyed the storehouses and brought dire famine upon the city.

A certain noble lady, Miriam, the daughter of Baythus, sent her servant to purchase some flour for household use. The servant found that all the flour had been sold, but there was still some meal which he might have purchased. Hurrying home, however, to learn his mistress's wishes in regard to this, he discovered on his return that this too had been sold, and he could obtain nothing save some coarse barley meal. Not wishing to purchase this without orders he returned home again, but when he returned to the store-house to secure the barley meal, that was gone also. Then his mistress started out herself to purchase food, but she could find nothing. Suffering from the pangs of hunger she picked from the street the skin of a fig and ate it; this sickened her and she died. But previous to her death she cast all her gold and silver into the street, saying, "What use is this wealth to me when I can obtain no food for it?" Thus were the words of Ezekiel fulfilled:

"Their silver shall they cast into the streets."

After the destruction of the storehouses, Rabbi Jochanan in walking through the city saw the populace boiling straw in water and drinking of the same for sustenance. "Ah, woe is me for this calamity!" he exclaimed; "how can such a people strive against a mighty host?" He applied to Ben Batiach, his nephew, one of the chiefs of the city, for permission to leave Jerusalem. But Ben Batiach replied, "It may not be; no living body may leave the city." Take me out then as a corpse," entreated Jochanan. Ben Batiach assented to this, and Jochanan was placed in a coffin and carried through the gates of the city; Rabbi Eleazer, Rabbi Joshua, and Ben Batiach acting as pallbearers. The coffin was placed in a cave, and after they had all returned to their homes Jochanan arose from the coffin and made his way to the enemy's camp. He obtained from the commander permission to establish an academy in Jabna with Rabbon Gamliel as the principal.

Titus soon captured the city, killed many of the people, and sent the others into exile. He entered the Temple, even in the Most Holy, and cut down the veil which separated it from the less sacred precincts. He seized the holy vessels, and sent them to Rome.

From this history of Kamtzah and Bar Kamtzah we should learn to be careful of offending our neighbors, when in so slight a cause such great results may originate. Our Rabbis have said that he who causes his neighbor to blush through an insult, should be compared to the one who sheds blood.

Hannah and her Seven Sons

During the terrible times which followed the fall of the Holy City, Hannah and her seven sons were cast into prison.

According to their ages they were brought before the tyrant conqueror, and commanded to pay homage to him and his gods.

"God forbid," exclaimed the eldest lad, "that I should bow to thy image. Our commandments say to us, 'I am the Lord thy God,' to no other will I bow."

He was immediately led out to execution, and the same demand made of his brother, the second son.

"My brother bowed not," he answered, "and no more will I."

"Wherefore not?" asked the tyrant.

"Because," replied the lad, "the second commandment of the Decalogue tells us, 'Thou shalt have no other God but me.' "

His death followed immediately his brave words.

"My religion teaches me, 'Thou shalt worship no other God' " (Ex. 34: 14), said the third son, "and I welcome the fate accorded to my brothers rather than bow to thee or thy images."

The same homage was demanded of the fourth son, but brave and faithful as his brethren, he replied, " 'He that sacrificeth unto any God save unto the Lord only' " (Ex. 22: 19), and was slain pitilessly.

" 'Hear, O Israel! the Lord our God, the Lord is One,' " exclaimed the fifth lad, yielding up his young life with the watchword of Israel's hosts.

"Why art thou so obstinate?" was asked of the sixth brother, when he, too, was brought before the tyrant and scorned the propositions made him.

" 'The Lord thy God is in the midst of thee, a mighty and terrible God' " (Deut. 7: 21), he said; and died for the principles he proclaimed.

Then the seventh and youngest boy was brought before the murderer of his relatives, who addressed him kindly, saying:

"My son, come bow before my gods."

And the child answered:

"God forbid! Our holy religion teaches us 'Know therefore this day, and reflect in thy heart that the Lord he is God, in the heavens above and on the earth beneath there is none else' (Deut. 4: 39). Never will we exchange our God for any other, neither will He exchange us for any other nation, for as it is written, 'Thou hast this day acknowledged the Lord' (Deut. 26: 17), so is it also written, 'And the Lord hath acknowledged thee this day, that thou art unto him a peculiar people!' "

Still the tyrant spoke smoothly, and with kind words.

"Thou art young," he said; "thou hast seen but little of the pleasures and joys of life, not as much as has fallen to the portion of thy brethren. Do as I wish thee and thy future shall be bright and happy."

"The Lord will reign for ever and ever," said the lad;

"thy nation and thy kingdom will be destroyed; thou art here today, tomorrow in the grave; today elevated, tomorrow lowly; but the most Holy One endures forever."

"See," continued the other, "thy brothers lie slain before thee; their fate will be thine if thou refusest to do as I desire. See, I will cast my ring to the ground, stoop thou and pick it up; that I will consider allegiance to my gods."

"Thinkest thou that I fear thy threats?" returned the unterrified lad; "why should I fear a human being more than the great God, the King of kings?"

"Where and what is thy God?" asked the oppressor. "Is there a God in the world?"

"Can there be a world without a Creator?" replied the youth. "Of thy gods 'tis said, 'mouths they have, but speak not.' Of our God the Psalmist says, 'By the word of the Lord were the heavens made.' Thy gods have 'eyes but see not,' but 'the eyes of the Lord run to and fro in the whole earth!' Thy gods have 'ears but hear not,' but of our God 'tis written, 'The Lord hearkened and heard.' Of thy gods 'tis said, 'a nose they have but smell not,' while our God 'smelled the sweet savor.' 'Hands have thy gods but they touch not,' while our God says, 'My hand hath also founded the earth.' Of thy gods 'tis written, 'feet they have but walk not,' while Zachariah tells us of our God, 'His feet will stand that day upon the mount of Olives.' "

Then said the cruel one:

"If thy God hath all these attributes, why does He not deliver thee from my power?"

The lad replied:

"He delivered Chananyah and his companions from the power of Nebuchadnezzar, but they were righteous men, and Nebuchadnezzar was a king deserving of seeing a miracle performed, but for me, alas, I am not worthy of redemption, neither art thou worthy of a demonstration of God's power."

"Let the lad be slain as were his brothers," commanded the tyrant.

Then spoke Hannah, the mother of the boys:

"Give me my child," she cried, "oh, cruel king, let me fold him in my arms ere thou destroyest his innocent young life."

She threw her arms around the lad, clasping him tightly to her bosom, and pressing her lips to his. "Take my life," she cried; "kill me first before my child."

"Nay," he answered, scoffingly, "I cannot do it, for thy own laws forbid; 'Whether it be ox or sheep ye shall not kill it and its young in one day' " (Lev. 28).

"Oh, woe to thee," replied the mother, "thou who art so particular to regard the laws." Then pressing her boy to her heart, "Go, my dear one," she said, "say to Abraham that my sacrifice hath exceeded his. He built one altar whereon to sacrifice Isaac; thy mother hath built seven altars and sacrificed seven Isaacs in one day. He was but tempted; thy mother hath performed."

After the execution of her last son, Hannah became insane, and threw herself from her house-top. Where she fell, she expired.

Happy are ye, ye seven sons of Hannah; your portion in the future world was waiting for you. In faithfulness ye served your God, and with her children shall your mother rejoice for ever in the eternal world.

CIVIL AND CRIMINAL LAW

"When do justice and goodwill meet? When the contending parties can be made to peaceably agree."

To accomplish this end was the great aim of the ancient Jewish laws, but a marked distinction was made between the civil and criminal branches. In the former cases, arguments could be made before, and decisions rendered by, either the general magistracy or special judges chosen by the contending parties, and many were the fences erected about the judges to keep them within the lines of strict equity, such as the following:

"He who unjustly transfers one man's goods to another shall answer to God for it with his own soul."

"When the judge sits in judgment on his fellow-man he should feel as though a sword was pointed at his heart."

"Woe to the judge who, knowing the unrighteousness of a decision, endeavors to make the witnesses responsible for the same. From *him* will God require an account."

"When the parties stand before thee look upon both as guilty; but when they are dismissed let them both be innocent, for the fiat has gone forth."

The judge was not allowed to hear anything of a case, save in the presence of all the parties concerned; and he was particularly enjoined to be without bias caused by a difference in the standing or wealth of the parties; either in favor of the poor against the rich, or of the rich against the poor.

The witnesses in a case were almost as closely scrutinized as the case itself, and they were at once incompetent if they had any personal interest in the suit. If a plaintiff asked for more than he was legally entitled to in the hope of more readily obtaining his due he lost his suit.

While three judges could form a tribunal for the settling of civil cases, that for the judgment of criminal suits was composed of twenty-three judges, and while in the former case a majority of one in the jury, either acquitted or condemned, in the latter a majority of one acquitted, but a majority of two was required to condemn.

The witnesses in criminal suits were thus admonished on being brought into court:

"Perchance you intend to speak from rumor, being the witness of another witness, to tell that which you have heard from a trustworthy man, or perchance you may not be aware that we shall try you with close questions and searching words. Know then, that trials wherein the life of man hangs in the scale, are not like trials concerning worldly goods. With money may money be redeemed, but in trials like this not only the blood of the one unjustly condemned, but that of his seed and his seed's seed, until the end of time, will lay heavy on the soul of the false witness. Adam was created alone one man, and he who destroys a single life will be held as accountable as if he had destroyed a world. Therefore search well thy words. But say not, on the other hand, 'What have I to do with all this?' Remember the words of Holy Writ, 'If a witness hath seen or known, if he do not utter, he shall bear his iniquity'; and remember further, 'In the destruction of the wicked there is joy.' "

The punishments were inflicted in the most humane manner, and the entire code is the perfection of justice tempered by mercy in its truest and highest sense.

No matter how numerous the crimes of an offender might be, one punishment covered them all. A fine could not accompany any other punishment, and in cases of flagellation, the number of strokes was limited in the most extreme cases to thirty-nine.

The judges in capital cases were required to fast all day on the days when they pronounced judgments, and even after the sentence the case was again considered by the highest court before it was carried into effect.

The place of execution was located a considerable distance from the court, and on his progress thereto the prisoner was stopped several times, and asked whether he could think of anything not said which might influence the judges in his favor. He had the privilege of returning to the court as often as he pleased with new pleas, and a herald preceded him, crying aloud, "This man is being led to execution, this is his crime . . . these are the witnesses against him . . . if any one knows aught in his favor let them come forth now and speak the words."

Before his execution he was urged to confess. "Confess thy sins," said the officers; "every one who confesses has part in the world to come." If he offered no confession he was requested to repeat the words, "May my death be a redemption for all my sins."

Capital punishment, however, was of such rare occurrence as to be practically abrogated. In fact, many of the judges declared openly for its abolition, and a court which had pronounced one sentence of death in seven years was called "the court of murderers."

THE HOLY DAYS

Passover

The feast of unleavened bread, or "Passover," begins upon the evening of the 14th day of *Nissan* (April), and was instituted in commemoration of our ancestors' redemption from Egypt, a memorial for ever. During its continuance we are strictly forbidden the use of any leavened thing.

Moses said to the Israelites in the name of the Lord: "Draw out and take for yourselves a lamb," &c.

By the observance of this precept they would deserve well of God and He would redeem them, for when He spoke they were "naked and bare" of good deeds and meritorious acts.

"Draw out and take for yourselves a lamb."

Draw yourselves away from the idols which ye are worshipping with the Egyptians, the calves and lambs of stone and metal, and with one of the same animals through which ye sin, prepare to fulfil the commandments of your God.

The planet sign of the month *Nissan* is a lamb; therefore, that the Egyptians might not think that through the powers of the lamb they had thrown off the yoke of slavery, God commanded His people to take a lamb and eat it.

They were commanded to roast it whole and to break no bone of it, so that the Egyptians might know that it was indeed a lamb which they had consumed.

The Lord said to Moses, "Tell the children of Israel that they shall borrow of the Egyptians gold and silver vessels," in order that it might not be afterwards said, "The words 'they will make them serve, and they will afflict them,' were fulfilled: but the words 'they shall go out with great substance,' did not come to pass."

When Moses told the Israelites that they should go up out of Egypt with great substance, they answered, "Would that we could go even empty-handed," like to the servant confined in prison.

"Tomorrow," said the jailer to him, "I will release thee from prison, and give thee much money."

"Let me go today, and give me nothing," replied the prisoner.

On the seventh day of the Passover the children of Israel passed through the Red Sea on dry land.

A man was once traveling along the road and his son preceded him on the way. A robber appeared in the path, and the man put his son behind him. Then lo, a wolf came after the lad, and his father lifted him up and carried him within his arms.

The sea was before the Israelites, the Egyptians were behind them, so God lifted up His child and carried it within His arms.

When Israel suffered from the hot rays of the sun God "spread the cloud for a covering"; when they were hungry He sent them bread from heaven; and when they thirsted "He brought forth floods from a rock."

Pentecost

The Feast of Weeks, or "Pentecost," occurs upon the sixth day of the third month, *Sivan* (June). It is called the Feast of Weeks because forty-nine days, or seven weeks, duly numbered, elapse between the second day of Passover, when (during the existence of the Temple) a sheaf of green barley was offered, and this festival, when two loaves made of the first flour of the wheat harvest were "brought before the Lord." It is also the anniversary of the delivery of the commandment from Mount Sinai.

Why does not the Bible particularize in this as on other occasions, and say directly, "On the sixth day of the third month was the law given"?

Because in ancient times the men called "wise" placed their faith and dependence upon the planets. They divided these into seven, apportioning one to each day of the week. Some nations selected for their greatest god the sun, other nations the moon, and so on, and prayed to them and worshipped them. They knew not that the planets moved and changed according to the course of nature, established by the Most High, a course which He might change according to His will, and into their ignorant ideas many of the Israelites had entered. Therefore, as they considered the planets as seven, God made many other things depending on that number, to show that as He made them, so had He made the planets.

The seventh day of the week He made the Sabbath; the seventh year he made the year of rest; after seven times seven years, or after seven Sabbatical years, He ordained the Jubilee, or year of release. Seven days He gave to the Passover festival, and seven days to the Feast of Tabernacles. Seven days was Jericho surrounded, and seven priests took seven trumpets and marched round its walls seven times upon the seventh day.

Therefore, after numbering seven weeks during the ripening time of the grain, the Israelites were to hold a holy convocation, to praise the One who can prevent all things, but who cannot be prevented; who can change all things, but is unchangeable.

The first day the Israelites were redeemed from slavery and superstition; the fiftieth day a law was given them for

their guide through life; therefore they are commanded
to number these days and remember them.

The children of Ishmael, says the legend, were asked
to accept the law. "What does it contain?" they asked.
"Thou shalt not steal," was the answer. "How can we
then accept it," they returned, "when thus was our fore-
father blessed, 'Thy hand shall be against every man'?"

The children of Esau were asked to accept the law, and
they also inquired, "What does it contain?" "Thou shalt
not kill," was the answer. "We cannot accept it, then,"
said they, "for thus did our father Isaac bless us, 'By the
sword shalt thou live.'"

When Israel was asked to accept the law, the people answered, "We will do and obey."

New Year, or the Day of Memorial

On the first day of the seventh month, *Tishri* (October), is the commemoration of the creation of the world.
Then the cornet is blown to announce to the people that
a new year has begun its course, and to warn them to
examine strictly their conduct and make amends therein
where amends are needed.

Would not any person of sense, knowing that he must
appear before a Court of Judgment, prepare himself therefor? Either in a civil or a criminal case would he not seek
for counsel? How much more, then, is it incumbent upon
him to prepare for a meeting with the King of kings, before whom all things are revealed. No counsel can help
him in his case; repentance, devotion, charity, these are
the arguments which must plead in his favor. Therefore, a
person should search his actions and repent his transgressions previous to the day of judgment. In the month of
Elul (September) he should arouse himself to a consciousness of the dread justice awaiting all mankind.

This is the season when the Lord pardoned the Israelites

who had worshipped the molten calf. He commanded Moses to reascend the mount for a second tablet, after he had destroyed the first. Thus say the sages, "The Lord said unto Moses in the month Elul, 'Go up unto me on the mountain,' and Moses went up and received the second tablet at the end of forty days. Before he ascended he caused the trumpet to be sounded through the camp." Since that time it is customary to sound the *Shophar* (cornet) in the synagogues, to give warning to the people that the day of judgment, New Year, is rapidly approaching, and with it the Day of Atonement. Therefore, propitiatory prayers are said twice every day, morning and evening, from the second day of Elul until the eve of the Day of Atonement, which period comprises the last forty days which Moses passed on Sinai, when God was reconciled to Israel and pardoned their transgressions with the molten calf.

Rabbi Eleazer said, "Abraham and Jacob were born in *Tishri,* and in *Tishri* they died. On the first of *Tishri* the universe was created, and during the Passover was Isaac born. On the first of *Tishri* (New Year), Sarah, Rachel, and Hannah, three barren women, were visited. On the first day of *Tishri* our ancestors discontinued their rigorous labor in Egypt. On the first of *Tishri* Adam was created; from his existence we count our years, that is the sixth day of the creation. On that day, too, did he eat of the forbidden fruit, therefore is the season appointed for one of penitence, for the Lord said to Adam, 'This shall be for a sign in future generations; thy descendants shall be judged upon these days, and they shall be appointed as days of pardon and forgiveness.' "

Four times in the year the Lord pronounces His decrees.

First, New Year, the first of *Tishri*. Then the judgments of all human beings for the coming year are ordained.

Second, The first day of Passover. Then the scarcity or fulness of the crops is determined.

Third, Pentecost. Then the Lord blesses the fruit of the trees, or bids them bear not in plenty.

Fourth, The Feast of Tabernacles. Then the Lord determines whether the rain shall bless the earth in its due season or not.

Man is judged on New Year's, and the decree is made final on the Day of Atonement.

Rabbi Nathan has said that man is judged at all times. Thus taught Rabbi Akiba. "Why does the law command the bringing of a sheaf of barley on the Passover? Because the Passover is the season of the harvest of the grain. The Lord says, 'Offer for me a sheaf of barley on Passover, that I may bless the grain which is in the field.'

"Why does the Bible say, 'Bring two loaves of the new wheat on Pentecost'? Because at Pentecost time the fruit ripens, and God says, 'Offer for me two loaves of the new wheat, in order that I may bless the fruit which is on the trees.'

"Why were we commanded to bring a drink-offering of water into the Temple on the Feast of Tabernacles? Because then is the season of rain, and the Lord says, 'Bring the drink-offering of water to me, in order that I may bless the rain of the year.'

"Why do they make the cornet which they blow of a ram's horn? In order that the Lord may remember the ram which was sacrificed instead of Isaac, and allow the merits of the patriarchs to weigh in favor of their descendants, as it is written in the Decalogue, 'Showing mercy to thousands of those who love me and keep my commandments' " (Ex. 20: 6).

On New Year's day they recite in the synagogues the record of the binding of Isaac for the same purpose.

While God has mercy upon His creatures He gives them a season for repentance, that they may not perish in their wickedness, therefore as it is written in Lamentations 3: 40, we should "search through and investigate our ways and return unto the Lord."

During the year man is apt to grow callous as to his transgressions, therefore the cornet is sounded to arouse him to the consciousness of the time which is passing so rapidly away. "Rouse thee from thy sleep," it says to him; "the hour of thy visitation approaches." The Eternal wishes not to destroy His children, merely to arouse them to repentance and good resolves.

Three classes of people are arraigned for judgment: the righteous, the wicked, and the indifferent. To the righteous the Lord awards a happy life; the wicked He condemns, and to the indifferent ones He grants a respite. From New Year's day until the Day of Atonement His judgment He holds in abeyance; if they repent truly they are classed with the righteous for a happy life, and if they remain untouched, they are counted with the wicked.

Three sounds for the cornet are commanded in the Bible. A pure sound (*T'kiah*), a sound of alarm or trembling (*T'ruah*), and, thirdly, a pure sound again (*T'kiah*).

The first sound typifies man's first awakening to penitence; he must search well his heart, desert his evil ways, and purify his thoughts, as it is written, "Let the wicked forsake his ways and the man of unrighteousness his thoughts, and let him return unto the Lord."

The alarm sound typifies the sorrow which a repentant man feels for his misconduct and his earnest determination to reform.

The last sound is the pure sound again, which typifies a sincere resolve to keep the repentant heart incorrupt.

The Bible says to us:

"The word is very nigh unto thee, in thy mouth and in thy heart, that thou mayest do it" (Deut. 30: 14). This verse teaches us that repentance is nearer to those who believe in God and His book than fanatics would make it. Difficult penances are ordained for the sinner among them. He must fast many days, or travel barefoot through rugged ways, or sleep in the open air. But we are not required to travel to the nether end of the ocean or to climb to mountain tops, for our Holy Word says to us, "It is not in heaven, neither is it beyond the sea, but the Word is very nigh."

In three ways may we repent:

First, By words of mouth, finding birth in an honest heart.

Secondly, With our feelings, sorrow for sins committed.

Thirdly, By good deeds in the future.

Rabbi Saadiah declared that God commanded us to sound the cornet on New Year's day for ten reasons.

First, Because this day is the beginning of the creation, when God began to reign over the world, and as it is customary to sound the trumpets at the coronation of a king, we should in like manner proclaim by the sound of the cornet that the Creator is our king—as David said, "With trumpets and the sound of the cornet, shout ye before the Lord."

Secondly, As the New Year day is the first of the ten penitential days, we sound the cornet as a proclamation to admonish all to return to God and repent. If they do not so, they at least have been informed, and cannot plead ignorance. Thus we find that earthly kings publish their decrees with such concomitant, that none may say, "We heard not this."

Thirdly, To remind us of the law given on Mouth Sinai, where it is said (Exod. 19: 16), "The voice of the cornet was exceeding loud." To remind us also that we should bind ourselves anew to the performance of its precepts, as did our ancestors, when they said, "All that the Lord hath said will we do and obey."

Fourthly, To remind us of the prophets, who were compared to watchmen blowing the trumpet of alarm, as we find in Ezekiel (33: 4), "Whosoever heareth the sound of the cornet and taketh not warning, and the sound cometh and taketh him away, his blood shall be upon his own head; but he that taketh warning shall save his life."

Fifthly, To remind us of the destruction of the Temple and the fearsome sound of the battle-cry of our enemies. "Because thou hast heard, oh my soul, the sound of the trumpet, the alarm of war" (Jerem. 4: 19). Therefore when we hear the sound of the cornet we should implore God to rebuild the Temple.

Sixthly, To remind us of the binding of Isaac, who willingly offered himself for immolation, in order to sanctify the Holy Name.

Seventhly, That when we hear the terrifying sound, we may, through dread, humble ourselves before the Supreme Being, for it is the nature of these martial instruments to produce a sensation of terror, as the prophet Amos observes, "Shall a trumpet be blown in a city, and the people not to be terrified?"

Eighthly, To remind us of the great and terrible Day of Judgment, on which the trumpet is to be sounded, as we find in Zeph. (1: 14-16), "The great day of the Lord is near, and hasteneth much, a day of the trumpet and of shouting."

Ninthly, To remind us to pray for the time when the outcasts of Israel are to be gathered together, as promised in Isaiah (28: 13), "And it shall come to pass in that day, the great trumpet shall be sounded, and those shall come who were perishing in the land of Assyria."

Tenthly, To remind us of the resurrection of the dead,

and our firm belief therein. "Yea, all ye that inhabit the world, and that dwell on the earth, when the standard is lifted upon the mountain, behold, and when the trumpet is sounded, hear!" says the prophet Isaiah.

Therefore should we set our hearts to these seasons, and fulfil the precept that the Bible commands us, as it is written:

"And the Lord commanded us to do all the statutes . . . that it might be well with us at all times" (Deut. 11: 24).

The Day of Atonement

The hearts of all who fear God should tremble with the reflection that all the deeds of the creature are known to the Creator, and will be by Him accounted to them for good or evil. God is ready at all times to acknowledge true penitence; and of repentance there are seven degrees:

First, The righteous man, who repents his misconduct as soon as he becomes aware of his sin. This is the best and most complete.

Secondly, Of the man who has for some time led a life of sin, yet who, in the vigor of his days, gives over his evil ways and conquers his wrong inclinations. As Solomon has said, "Remember thy Creator in the days of thy youthful vigor" (Eccl. 12). While in the prime of life abandon thy evil ways.

Thirdly, Of the one who was prevented by some cause from the commission of a contemplated sin, and who truly repents his evil intention. "Happy is the man who fears the Lord," said the Psalmist. The man, not the woman? Aye, all mankind. The word is used to denote strength; those who repent while still in their youth.

Fourthly, Of the one who repents when his sin is pointed out to him, and he is rebuked for the same, as in the instance of the inhabitants of Nineveh. They repented not until Jonah proclaimed to them, "Yet forty days more, and Nineveh shall be overthrown" (Jonah 3: 4). The men of Nineveh believed in God's mercy, and though the decree had been pronounced against them, yet they repented. "And God saw their work, that they had returned from their evil ways, and God bethought Himself of the evil which He had spoken that He would do to them, and He did it not." Therefore say the Rabbis, "Our brethren, neither sackcloth nor fasting will gain forgiveness for sins; but repentance of the heart and good deeds; for it is not said of the men of Nineveh, "God saw their fasting and sackcloth," but "God saw their *work,* that they had turned from their evil ways."

Fifthly, Of those who repent when trouble befalls them. How much nobler is this than human nature! Instance Jephtah: "Did ye not hate me . . . and why are ye come unto me now when you are in distress?" (Judges 11: 8). But the infinite mercy of our God accepts even such repentance; as it is written, "When thou art in tribulation, and all these things have overtaken thee . . . then wilt thou return unto the Lord thy God." Founded upon this is the proverb of the fathers, "Repentance and good deeds form a shield against punishment."

Sixthly, The repentance of age. Even when man grows old and feeble, if he repents truly, his atonement will be received. As the Psalmist says, "Thou turnest man to contrition, and sayest, 'Return, ye children of men.' " Meaning, man can return at any time or any age, "Return, ye children of men."

Say the Rabbis, "Although a man has been righteous in his youth and vigor, yet if he rebels against the will of God in his old age, the merit of his former goodness shall be lost to him, as it is written, 'When a righteous man turns away from his righteousness and doeth wrong, and dieth therefor; through his wrong which he hath done must he die' (Ezekiel 18: 26). But a man who has been wicked in his early days, and feels true sorrow and penitence in his old age, shall not be called 'wicked' any more. This, however, is not gracious penitence when it is so long delayed."

Seventhly, Is the last degree of penitence. Of the one who is rebellious against his Creator during all the days of his life; turns to Him only when the hand of death is laid upon him.

Say the Rabbis, if a person is sick, and the hour of his decease approaches, they who are by his deathbed should say to him, "Confess thy sins to thy Creator."

They who are near the point of death should confess their shortcomings. The sick man is as the man who is before a court of justice. The latter may have advocates to defend him or laud his case, but the only advocates of the former must be penitence and good deeds. As is written in the Book of Job (33: 23), "If there be now about him one single angel as defender, one out of a thousand, to tell for man his uprightness; then is he gracious unto him, and saith, 'Release him from going down to the pit; I have found an atonement.'"

Thus we have seven different degrees of penitence, and he who neglects them all must suffer in the world to come. Therefore fulfil the duties laid upon you; repent as long as you are able to amend. As the Rabbis say, "Repent in the antechamber, that thou mayest enter the room of state."

"Turn ye, turn ye from your evil ways; wherefore will ye die, O house of Israel!" exclaimed the prophet Ezekiel; and what does this warning mean? without repentance ye shall die.

Penitence is thus illustrated by a parable:

There was once a great ship which had been sailing for many days upon the ocean. Before it reached its destination, a high wind arose, which drove it from its course; until, finally, becalmed close to a pleasant-appearing island, the anchor was dropped. There grew upon this island beautiful flowers and luscious fruits in "great profusion"; tall trees lent a pleasing, cooling shade to the place, which appeared to the ship's passengers most desirable and inviting. They divided themselves into five parties; the first party determined not to leave the ship, for said they, "A fair wind may arise, the anchor may be raised, and the ship sail on, leaving us behind; we will not risk the chance of missing our destination for the temporary pleasure which this island offers." The second party went on shore for a short time, enjoyed the perfume of the flowers, tasted of the fruit, and returned to the ship happy and refreshed, finding their places as they had left them; losing nothing, but rather gaining in health and good spirits by the recreation of their visit on shore. The third party also visited the island, but they stayed so long that the fair wind did arise, and hurrying back they just reached the ship as the sailors were lifting the anchor, and in the haste and confusion many lost their places, and were not as comfortable during the balance of their voyage as at the outset. They were wiser, however, than the fourth party; these latter stayed so long upon the island and tasted so deeply of its pleasures, that they allowed the ship's bell of warning to sound unheeded. Said they, "The sails are still to be set; we may enjoy ourselves a few minutes more." Again the bell sounded, and still they lingered, thinking, "The captain will not sail without us." So they remained on shore until they saw the ship moving; then in wild haste they swam after it and scrambled up the sides, but the bruises and injuries which they encountered in so doing were not healed during the remainder of the voyage. But, alas, for the fifth party. They ate and drank so deeply that they did not even hear the bell, and when the ship started they were left behind. Then the wild beasts hid in the thickets made of them a prey, and they who escaped this evil, perished from the poison of surfeit.

The "ship" is our good deeds, which bear us to our destination, heaven. The "island" typifies the pleasures of the world, which the first set of passengers refused to taste or look upon, but which when enjoyed temperately, as by the second party, make our lives pleasant, without causing us to neglect our duties. These pleasures must not be allowed, however, to gain too strong a hold upon our senses. True, we may return, as the third party, while there is yet time and but little bad effect, or even as the fourth party at the eleventh hour, saved, but with bruises and injuries which cannot be entirely healed; but we are in danger of becoming as the last party, spending a lifetime in the pursuit of vanity, forgetting the future, and perishing even of the poison concealed in the sweets which attracted us.

Who hath sorrow? Who hath woe?

He who leaves much wealth to his heirs, and takes with him to the grave a burden of sins. He who gathers wealth without justice. "He that gathereth riches and not by right (Jer. 8: 11), in the midst of his days shall he leave them." To the portals of eternity his gold and his silver cannot accompany the soul of man; good deeds and trust in God must be his directing spirits.

Although God is merciful and pardons the sins of man against Himself, he who has wronged his neighbor must gain that neighbor's forgiveness before he can claim the mercy of the Lord. "This must ye do," said Rabbi Eleazer, "that ye may be clean from all your sins before the Lord

(Lev. 16: 30). The Day of Atonement may gain pardon for the sins of man against his Maker, but not for those against his fellow-man, till every wrong done is satisfied."

If a man is called upon to pardon his fellow, freely he must do it; else how can he dare, on the Day of Atonement, to ask pardon for his sins against the Eternal? It is customary on this day for a man to thoroughly cleanse himself bodily and spiritually, and to array himself in white fresh clothing, to typify the words of Isaiah, "Though your sins should be as scarlet, they shall become white as snow."

It happened that the mayor of a city once sent his servant to the market to purchase some fish. When he reached the place of sale he found that all the fish save one had been sold, and this one a Jewish tailor was about purchasing. Said the mayor's servant, "I will give one gold piece for it"; said the tailor, "I will give two." The mayor's messenger then expressed his willingness to pay three gold pieces for it, but the tailor claimed the fish, and said he would not lose it though he should be obliged to pay ten gold pieces for it. The mayor's servant then returned home, and in anger related the circumstance to his master. The mayor sent for his subject, and when the latter appeared before him asked:

"What is thy occupation?"

"A tailor, sir," replied the man.

"Then how canst thou afford to pay so great a price for a fish, and how dare degrade my dignity by offering for it a larger sum than that offered by my servant?"

"I fast tomorrow," replied the tailor, "and I wished the fish to eat today, that I might have strength to do so. I would not have lost it even for ten pieces of gold."

"What is tomorrow more than any other day?" asked the mayor.

"Why art thou more than any other man?" returned the other.

"Because the king hath appointed me to this office."

"Well," replied the tailor, "the King of kings hath appointed this day to be holier than all other days, for on this day we hope that God will pardon our transgressions."

"If this be the case thou wert right," answered the mayor, and the Israelite departed in peace.

Thus if a person's intention is to obey God, nothing can hinder its accomplishment. On this day God commanded His children to fast, but they must strengthen their bodies to obey him by eating on the day before. It is a person's duty to sanctify himself, bodily and spiritually, for the approach of this great day. He should be ready to enter at any moment into the Fearful Presence with repentance and good deeds as his companions.

A certain man had three friends. One of these he loved dearly; the second he loved also, but not as intensely as the first; but towards the third one he was quite indifferently disposed.

Now the king of the country sent an officer to this man, commanding his immediate appearance before the throne. Greatly terrified was the man at this summons. He thought that somebody had been speaking evil of him, or probably accusing him falsely before his sovereign, and being afraid to appear unaccompanied before the royal presence, he resolved to ask one of his friends to go with him. First he naturally applied to his dearest friend, but he at once declined to go, giving no reason and no excuse for his lack of friendliness. So the man applied to his second friend, who said to him:

"I will go with thee as far as the palace gates, but I will not enter with thee before the king."

In desperation the man applied to his third friend, the

one whom he had neglected, but who replied to him at once:

"Fear not; I will go with thee, and I will speak in thy defence. I will not leave thee until thou art delivered from thy trouble."

The "first friend" is a man's wealth, which he must leave behind him when he dies. The "second friend" is typified by the relatives who follow him to the grave and leave him when the earth has covered his remains. The "third friend," he who entered with him into the presence of the king, is as the good deeds of a man's life, which never desert, but accompany him to plead his cause before the King of kings, who regardeth not person nor taketh bribery.

Thus taught Rabbi Eleazer:

"On this great and tearful day the angel Samal finds no blots, no sins on Israel." Thus he addresses the Most High:

" 'O Sovereign Lord, upon the earth this day one nation pure and innocent exists. Even as the angels is Israel on this Atonement Day. As peace exists in heaven, so rests it now upon this people, praying to Thy Holy Name.'

"God hears this testimony of His angel, and pardons all His people's sins."

But though the Almighty thus forgives our sins, we may not repeat them with impunity, for "to such a one as saith, 'I will commit a sin and repent,' there can be no forgiveness, no repentance."

Feast of Tabernacles

The Feast of Tabernacles begins on the fifteenth day of the seventh month, *Tishri* (October), and during its continuance, seven days, the Israelites are commanded to dwell in tabernacles or booths. This is designed to keep fresh in their memory the tents which formed their homes during their forty years' sojourn in the wilderness. The symbols of the festival are branches of the palm, bound with sprigs of myrtle and willow, and a citron.

On this feast we are commanded to rejoice and be glad, for it is not the desire of God that we should always afflict ourselves as upon His precious holy day, the Day of Atonement. No; after humbling our hearts and returning to our Creator, we are enjoined to rejoice with our families and neighbors; therefore, we call this holy day the season of our rejoicing.

The Lord said, "This is not to be to you a fast as the Day of Atonement; eat, drink, be merry, and sacrifice peace-offerings thereon." The Bible says, "Seven days unto the Lord"; therefore we should in all our merriment devote a few serious thoughts to Him.

The Omnipotent King has commanded us to remove from our permanent dwellings and live for seven days in booths. This precept teaches us that man should put no trust in the magnificent structures he may have raised and adorned with ornaments of value, nor to place his confidence entirely upon human beings, even though rulers in his land; but to rely solely upon the Almighty, the One who said, "Let the universe come into being"; to Him alone is the power and the dominion. He alone will never change, or be other than He has proclaimed Himself, as it is written, "God is not a man that He should lie" (Num. 23: 19), and He alone can prove our sure protection.

The Feast of Tabernacles is held in the autumn, after the fruits of the field have been garnered in the storehouses, according to the words of the Bible, "The Feast of Tabernacles shalt thou hold for thyself seven days when thou hast gathered in the produce of thy threshing-floor and thy wine press" (Deut. 16: 14).

At this time, when a man sees plenty around him, his heart perhaps may grow haughty, he may feel like enriching his house and furnishing it with elegance; for this reason he is commanded to leave it for a season, and dwell in booths, where his thoughts may be directed to God. That in the dwelling rudely put together, and unprotected from the rain, he may remember that through the rain sent by the Most High in its due season did the profusion of his crops result, and with this reflection appreciate the fact that all he possesses he owes to the goodness of God, and not to his own intelligence or strength.

This dwelling in booths is also to bring to mind the manner in which the Israelites lived for forty years after they left Egypt. With merely temporary walls to protect them from summer's heat and winter's cold, from wind and storm. God was with them through all their generations, and they were protected from all evil.

According to the opinion of some of the Rabbis, the Israelites did not really dwell in booths in the wilderness, but were surrounded by clouds—by seven clouds. Four clouds, one at each of the four sides; a fifth, a shadow, to protect them from the hot rays of the sun; the sixth, a pillar of fire, to give them light by night (they being able to see as clearly by night as by day); and the seventh, to precede their journeying and direct their way.

The children of Israel departed from Egypt in *Nissan* (April), and obtained immediately these booths, which they made use of for forty years. Thus they were in booths during the entire cycle of the year, and we could as easily commemorate this fact in the spring as in the fall, in the summer as in the winter. Why, then, has God made autumn, and neither spring nor summer, the season of observance? Because if we dwelt in booths in the summer, it would be a question whether we did so in obedience to God's behest or for our own gratification; for many people seek airy retreats during this season; but in the fall, when the trees lose their leaves, and the air grows cold and chilling, and it is the time to fix our houses for the winter, then by inhabiting these temporary residences, we display our desire to do as our Creator has bidden us.

The Feast of Tabernacles is also the Feast of Ingathering, when we should thank God for the kindness shown us, and the treasure with which He has blessed us. When the Eternal has provided man with his sustenance, in the long evenings which follow he should meditate and study his Bible, and make this indeed a "feast to the Lord," and not entirely for personal gratification.

The four species belonging to the vegetable kingdom, which we use on this festival, are designed to remind us of the four elements of nature, which work under the direction and approval of the Most High, and without which all things would cease to exist. Therefore the Bible commands us on this "feast of the Lord" to give thanks, and bring before Him these four species, each typifying one of the elements.

"Ye shall take for yourselves (Lev. 23: 40) the fruit of the tree *hadar*" (the citron). Its color is high yellow and resembles fire. The second species is the palm branch (Heb. *Lulab*). The palm is a high tree, growing up straight in the air, and its fruit is sweet and delicious to the taste; this then represents the second element, air. The third is the bough of the myrtle, one of the lowliest of trees, growing close to the ground; its nature, cold and dry as earth, fits it to represent that element. The fourth is "the willow of the brook," which grows in perfection close beside the water, dropping its branches into the stream, and symbolizing thus the last element, water.

The Bible teaches us that for each of these four elements we owe especial thanks to God.

The citron we hold in the left hand, and the other three we grasp together in the right. This we do because the citron contains in itself all that the others represent. The outside skin is yellow, fire; the inside skin is white and damp, air; the pulp is watery, water; and the seeds are dry, earth. It is taken into the left hand, because the right hand is strongest, and the citron is but one, while the other emblems are three.

These four emblems represent likewise the four principal members of the human body. The citron is shaped somewhat like a heart, without which we could not live, and with which man should serve his fellows; the palm branch represents the spine, which is the foundation of the human frame, in front of which the heart lies; this signifies that we should serve God with our entire body. The branches of the myrtle resemble a human eye, with which man recognizes the deeds of his fellows, and with which he may obtain a knowledge of the law. The leaves of the willow represent the lips, with which man may serve the Eternal and thank Him. The myrtle is mentioned in the Bible before the willow, because we are able to see and know a thing before we can call its name with our lips; man is able to look into the Bible before he can study the same. Therefore, with these four principal parts of the human frame should we praise the Creator, as David said, "All my bones shall say, O Lord, who is like unto thee?"

The great Maimonides, in his work called *"Moreh Nebuchim"* (The Guide of the Perplexed), explains that God commanded the Israelites to take these four emblems during this festival to remind them that they were brought out from the wilderness, where no fruit grew, and no people lived, into a land of brooklets, waters, a land flowing with milk and honey. For this reason did God command us to hold in our hands the precious fruit of this land while singing praises to Him, the One who wrought miracles in our behalf, who feeds and supports us from the productiveness of the earth.

The four emblems are different in taste, appearance, and odor, even as the sons of men are different in conduct and habits.

The citron is a valuable fruit; it is good for food and has a most pleasant odor. It is compared to the intelligent man, who is righteous in his conduct towards God and his fellow-man. The odor of the fruit is his good deeds; its substance is his learning, on which others may feed. This is perfect among the emblems, and is, therefore, always mentioned first, and taken by itself in one hand.

The palm branch brings forth fruit, but is without odor. It is compared to those people who are learned, but who are wanting in good deeds; they who know the law, but transgress its mandates.

The myrtle is compared to those people who are naturally good, who act correctly towards God and man, but who are uneducated.

The willow of the brook has neither fruit nor odor; it is, therefore, compared to the people who have no knowledge and who perform no good deeds.

If all unite together, however, and offer supplication to the Most High, He will surely hearken to their words, and for this reason Moses said to the Israelites, "And ye shall take unto yourselves," &c.; meaning, to your own benefit, to praise the Lord during the seven days of the festival with these emblems, and to exclaim with the same *"Hoshaánah"* (O, save us now), and "Oh, give thanks to the Lord, for His mercy endureth for ever."

The Rabbis have said that he who has failed to participate in the keeping of the Tabernacle Festival in Jerusalem has failed to taste real enjoyment in his life. The first day of the feast was kept with great solemnity, and the middle days with joy and gladness in various methods of public amusement.

The Temple in Jerusalem was provided with a gallery for the women, which was called the apartment of the women, and the men sat below, as is still the custom of the synagogue. Thither all repaired. The young priests filled the lamps of the large chandeliers with oil, and lighted them all, even that the place was so bright that its reflection lighted the streets of the city. Hymns and praises were chanted by the pious ones, and the Levites praised the Lord with harps, cornets, trumpets, flutes, and other instruments of harmony. They stood upon fifteen broad steps, reaching from the lower floor to the gallery, the court of the women. And they sang fifteen psalms as they ascended, beginning with "A song of Degrees," and the large choir joined voices with them. The ancient Hillel was accustomed to address the assemblages on these occasions.

"If God's presence dwells here," he was used to say, "then are ye here, each one of you, the souls of each; but if God should be removed from your midst through disobedience then which of you could be here?" For the Lord has said, "If thou wilt come to My house, then will I come to thy house, but if thou refusest to visit My dwelling, I will also neglect to enter yours"; as it is written,

"In every place where I shall permit My name to be mentioned I will come unto thee and I will bless thee" (Exod. xx. 21).

Then some of the people answered:

"Happy were the days of our youth, for they have not set to blush the days of our old age." These were men of piety.

Others answered:

"Happy is our old age, for therein have we atoned for the sins of our youth." These were repentants.

Then joining together, both parties said:

"Happy is the one who is free from sin; but ye who have sinned, repent, return to God, and ye will be forgiven."

The festival was continued during the entire night; for when the religious exercises concluded the people gave themselves up to innocent but thorough enjoyment.

This festival was also called the "Festival of Drawing Water."

Because, during the existence of the Temple, wine was offered during the year for a burnt-offering, but on the Feast of Tabernacles they offered two drink-offerings, one of wine and one of water. Of the other they made a special festival on the second day of the Tabernacle assemblage, calling it the Feast of Drawing the Water. It was founded upon the words of the prophet:

"And ye shall draw water with joy from the fountains of salvation."

Hannukah, the Feast of Dedication

This festival is observed for eight days during the ninth month *Kislev* (December), and commemorates the dedication of the Temple after it had been defiled by Antiochus Epiphanes, whose armies were overthrown by the valiant Maccabees, Hashmoneans.

The Most Holy One has frequently wrought wonders in behalf of his children in their hour of need, and thereby displayed His supreme power to the nations of the world. These should prevent man from growing infidel and ascribing all happiness to the course of nature. The God who created the world from naught, may change at His will the nature which He established. When the Hashmoneans gained, with the aid of God, their great victory, and restored peace and harmony to their land, their first act was to cleanse and rededicate the Temple, which had been defiled, and on the twenty-fifth day of Kislev, in obedience to the teachings of the Rabbis, we inaugurate the "Dedication Feast" by lighting the lamps or candles prepared expressly for this occasion. The first night we light one, and then an additional one each succeeding night of its continuance. We also celebrate it by hymns of thanksgiving and hallelujahs.

This feast is foreshadowed in the Book of Numbers. When Aaron observed the offerings of the princes of each of the tribes and their great liberality, he was conscious of a feeling of regret, because he and his tribe were unable to join with them. But these words were spoken to comfort him, "Aaron, thy merit is greater than theirs, for thou lightest and fixest the holy lamps."

When were these words spoken?

When he was charged with the blessing to be found in Numbers 6: 23, as will be found in the Book of Maccabees in the Apocrypha.

The Lord said unto Moses, "Thus say unto Aaron. In the generations to come, there will be another dedication and lighting of the lamps, and through thy descendants shall the service be performed. Miracles and wonders will accompany this dedication. Fear not for the greatness of the princes of thy tribe; during the existence of the Temple thou shalt sacrifice, but the lighting of the lamps shall be for ever, and the blessing with which I have charged thee to bless the people shall also exist for ever. Through the destruction of the Temple the sacrifices will be abolished, but the lighting of the dedication of the Hashmoneans will never cease."

The Rabbis have ordained this celebration by lighting of lamps, to make God's miracle known to all coming generations, and it is our duty to light the same in the synagogues and in our homes.

Although the Lord afflicted Israel on account of iniquities, He still showed mercy, and allowed not a complete destruction, and to this festival do the Rabbis again apply the verse in Leviticus 26: 44:

"And yet for all that, though they be in the land of their enemies, will I not cast them away, neither will I loathe them to destroy them utterly, to break my covenant with them, for I am the Lord their God."

And thus do the Rabbis explain the same:

"Will I not cast them away." In the time of the Chaldeans I appointed Daniel and his companions to deliver them.

"Neither will I loathe them." In the time of the Assyrians I gave them Matthias, his sons and their comrades, to serve them.

"To destroy them." In the time of Haman I sent Mordecai and Esther to rescue them.

"To break my covenant with them." In the time of the Romans I appointed Rabbi Judah and his associates to work their salvation.

"For I am the Eternal, your God." In the future no nation shall rule over Israel, and the descendants of Abraham shall be restored to their independent state.

The dedication commemorated by Hannukah occurred in the year 3632—129 B.C.E.

Purim

This festival, occurring on the fourteenth day of the twelfth month, *Adar* (March), is to commemorate the deliverance of the Hebrews from the wiles of Haman, through the God-aided means of Mordecai and Esther.

Although the Holy One threatens the Israelites, in order that they may repent of their sins, He has also tempted them, in order to increase their reward.

For instance, a father who loves his son, and desires him to improve his conduct, must punish him for his misdeeds; but it is a punishment induced by affection which he bestows.

A certain apostate once said to Rabbi Saphra:

"It is written, 'Because I know you more than all the nations of the earth, therefore I visit upon you your iniquities'; how is this? If a person has a wild horse, is it likely that he would put his dearest friend upon it, that he might be thrown and hurt?"

Rabbi Saphra answered:

"Suppose a man lends money to two persons; one of these is his friend, the other his enemy. He will allow his friend to repay him in instalments, that the discharge of the debt may not prove onerous; but from his enemy he will require the amount in full. The verse you quote will apply in the same manner, 'I love you, therefore will I visit upon you your iniquities'; meaning, 'I will punish you for them as they occur, little by little, by which means you may have quittance and happiness in the world to come.'"

The action of the king in delivering his signet ring to Haman had more effect upon the Jews than the precepts and warnings of forty-eight prophets who lectured to them early and late. They clothed themselves in sackcloth, and repented truly with tears and fasting, and God had compassion upon them and destroyed Haman.

Although the reading of the Book of Esther (*Megilah*) on Purim is not a precept of the Pentateuch, 'tis nevertheless binding upon us and our descendants. Therefore the day is appointed as one of feasting and gladness, and interchange of presents, and also of gifts to the poor, that they too may rejoice. As in the decree of Haman, no distinction was made between rich and poor, as all alike were doomed to destruction, it is proper that all should have equal cause to feel joyful, and therefore in all generations the poor should be liberally remembered on this day.